Presented To:

_____

From:

_____

Date:

_____

SECRETS

of the SUPERNATURAL

LIFE

SECRETS

of the SUPERNATURAL

LIFE

YOUR GATEWAY *to* SUPERNATURAL
EXPERIENCES

SHAWN GABIE

DESTINY IMAGE₍®₎ PUBLISHERS, INC.
P.O. Box 310, Shippensburg, PA 17257-0310
"Promoting Inspired Lives."

This book and all other Destiny Image, Revival Press, MercyPlace, Fresh Bread, Destiny Image Fiction, and Treasure House books are available at Christian bookstores and distributors worldwide.

For a U.S. bookstore nearest you, call **1-800-722-6774**.
For more information on foreign distributors, call **717-532-3040**.
Reach us on the Internet: **www.destinyimage.com.**

ISBN 13 TP: 978-0-7684-4120-8
ISBN 13 Ebook: 978-0-7684-8841-8

For Worldwide Distribution, Printed in the U.S.A.
1 2 3 4 5 6 7 8 / 16 15 14 13 12

Bio photograph by Kelly Logan.
Author page designed by JC Creative Business Solutions
Designed to Succeed.
jccreative.ca

DEDICATION

THIS book is dedicated first and foremost to making the name and person of Jesus Christ known to the world as the supernatural doorway to true spiritual life and experience. It is also dedicated to not only the hungry, faith-filled believer in Christ, but also the searching believer who knows there is more to spiritual life, as well as the one searching for truth and a genuine experience of the supernatural. Let Jesus Christ reveal Himself to you as the gateway to heavenly encounters and experience.

ACKNOWLEDGMENTS

FIRST I want to thank Holy Spirit for guiding me throughout my life to learn some of the nuts and bolts of operating in the supernatural. It's been an incredible journey. I also want to thank my amazing wife, Michelle, our two daughters, Promise Nevaeh and Victory Sage, and our child in the womb—they have truly sacrificed to allow me to write this book. I love you and am so glad I get to do life with all of you. May the fruit of this book bounce back at you and be nothing but a blessing to you. My prayer is that all my children would know the secrets of the supernatural life and live by these principles all the days of their lives.

I also would like to thank my mom who took time to do some editing; you are incredible. And thanks to all those at Destiny Image who helped me during this project. It was quite the process but worth it in the end. (And all those vanilla bean lattes and the great working atmosphere in the local coffee shop.) Lastly, I must thank all of the mentors and spiritual fathers and mothers in my life who have been so instrumental in steering and guiding me forward. To name a few, Wayne and Kristi Northup, Patricia King, Wesley and Stacey Campbell, and Bill and Gwen Prankard, your examples of faith and diligence have inspired and encouraged me along the way and will never be forgotten.

Endorsements

Shawn Gabie's *Secrets of the Supernatural Life* is a practical handbook on the prophetic that will teach you to connect Heaven to earth in your every day. Learn to hear the voice of God and then speak confidently. It is time we become His voice to the voiceless and bring supernatural change to hurting communities.

Rachel Hickson
Director, Heartcry for Change Ministries
Oxford, United Kingdom

We are living in a supernatural world. Every aspect of society—religion, media, education, even business—is being impacted by the spiritual world of psychics, prophets, and supernatural phenomena.

The good news is that there is an emerging body of people with a deep revelation of Jesus Christ, the true supernatural door to spiritual experiences; and this body of people is actively being deployed to reform society. God is raising up Daniels who will rule and reign and bring His Kingdom to earth (see Matt. 6:10). In this highly motivating book, *Secrets of the Supernatural Life*, Shawn Gabie gives a clear blueprint for why we need teaching and training in the supernatural, as well as practical tools on how to walk in the supernatural every day. If you are hungering for more of the supernatural in your life, you will *love* this book! We can attest that Shawn has personally put into practice all that he writes about. He is a great guy with a great message.

Wesley and Stacey Campbell
Revival Now Ministries / Be A HERO
Kelowna, British Columbia, Canada

Shawn's book, *Secrets of the Supernatural Life*, is a literary masterpiece—dangerous to spiritual mediocrity. The revelatory truths, practical tools, and strong biblical foundation laid out in this book will propel you into experiencing a supernatural lifestyle. Well done, Shawn!

Faisal Malick
Covenant of Life Ministries
Langley, British Columbia, Canada

For too long, fear of the unknown has impeded believers from stepping into authentic Kingdom living to experience the fullness of Heaven on earth. In *Secrets of the Supernatural Life*, Shawn Gabie demolishes old mindsets and challenges us to start functioning from a heavenly perspective. Every facet of culture, including religion, has been influenced—and in many cases, overtaken—by humanistic or demonic forces. The apostle Paul chided the Corinthian believers for being *"carnal* and behaving like mere men" (1 Cor. 3:3). This book shows you that you are not "mere" humans; you are empowered with the miracle-working, revelatory, limitless resources of the Kingdom to impact and transform your world. As you read, allow *Secrets of the Supernatural Life* to penetrate your heart, then step out and start demonstrating the Kingdom!

Bill Prankard
President, Bill Prankard Evangelistic Association
Pastor, Dominion Outreach Centre
Ottawa, Ontario, Canada

As an evangelist, pastor, and leader, I have become so aware of my limitations to properly minister the gospel. The supernatural power of God can't be my second option; it must be my priority. Shawn Gabie offers us the heart, insight, and tools on how to make the supernatural come into fullness in our lives. This is a must-read for all Christ followers hungering for God to do something out of the box in and through them.

Wayne Northup
President, Answering the Cries
Lead Pastor, Saints Community Church
New Orleans, Louisiana, United States

Secrets of the Supernatural Life is awesome—revelatory, deep, and yet totally power-packed with practical wisdom on how to walk out a supernatural life in Christ. If you have a hunger to understand the things of the Spirit in a biblically grounded way and then live it out in your everyday life, this book gives you the tools to get there! I love Shawn Gabie's revelatory teaching gift.

Faytene Grasseschi
Best-selling Author, Activist
Revivalist and Artist/TheCRY

We are in the midst of the most significant regime change in history. Shawn Gabie is a new breed of leader on the bleeding edge of this transition. It is no longer enough to just talk about the supernatural life. We must see every believer thoroughly equipped to manifest in his or her everyday life the realities of his or her supernatural inheritance. *Secrets of the Supernatural Life* is a significant piece of apostolic weaponry that is designed to empower the Body of Christ to demonstrate—here and now—the glory of the Kingdom to a desperate world. This book is the fruit of a proven supernatural practitioner. The revelation is clear and accurate and is accompanied with handles to ensure relevant application. Thank you, Shawn!

D. Karl Thomas
Senior Pastor, Impact Church
National Leader, The Apostolic Church in Canada
London, Ontario, Canada

This book is a great read for those who hunger for the reality of the Kingdom of God to be manifested in their lives on a daily basis. Shawn is a forerunner for the new breed of apostolic reformers God is raising up to help bring the church to the next level. No surface-y stuff here, this book dives into the deep end and takes you to the cutting edge of experiencing God for yourself. I highly recommend this book and believe it will impact and challenge you to walk in the fullness of all that God has called you to do and be.

Charlie Robinson
Revival Canada Christian Ministries
Dunham, Quebec

*God has privileged us in Christ Jesus to live
above the ordinary human plane of life.*

*Those who want to be ordinary and live on a lower place
can do so, but as for me, I will not.*

—Smith Wigglesworth

CONTENTS

FOREWORD

SHAWN Gabie's book, *Secrets of the Supernatural Life*, is a very timely work indeed. The masses today are increasingly intrigued by and hungry for spiritual things. An emphasis on materialism, career, and education in our society, for the most part, has left them feeling empty and longing for purpose in life. Many youth today are fearful of the future and yet are longing to give themselves to something meaningful. They often feel powerless next to the shakings around them.

Individuals of all ages are seeking something they can live for, something they can die for. Yet, education, family, career, material security, sexual fulfillment, church life, and escapism through the drug scene—these have all fallen short in satisfying the deep inner cries resident in most hungry hearts. Political activists have failed in offering national and global security; military forces are vulnerable; economic systems are shaky; and even the earth itself is regularly trembling with an increased frequency of earthquakes and natural disasters. As a result, we are seeing a growing emergence of spiritual hunger and awakening.

People everywhere are hungry for power and are consequently turning to the supernatural. Spiritual cults are increasing rapidly as the masses look for a Power greater than themselves. We are spiritual beings and deep inside we understand that there is a realm, a reality, and a dimension that is beyond ourselves of which we are a part. Unfortunately, religion and its parched, spiritless theology has very little to offer the hungry, modern person who seeks a spirituality that is high above the rationalism of our day.

Isaiah prophesied the following to a people who would arise in the midst of a dark day: *"Arise, shine; for your light has come! And the glory of the Lord is risen upon you"* (Isa. 60:1).

Isaiah was describing a company of radical, passionate believers, such as Shawn Gabie and company, who refuse to settle for the mundane. They are arising now. They are shining. The glory of the Lord is appearing upon them. They are true believers who embrace the full counsel of the Word of God. These passionate followers of Truth wholeheartedly believe that the same works Jesus did, they can do also—and they do.

In *Secrets of the Supernatural Life*, you will find insights and nuggets of wisdom that will stir fresh passion, faith, and focus in your life. You will find yourself hungering and thirsting for more of God, His Kingdom, and His righteousness. You will delight in the discovery of all the Lord reveals to you in regard to living a supernatural lifestyle in a very natural way. Let a new day begin for you. You are a supernatural being and are created for fullness in Christ. There is more for you—much, much more.

Patricia King
Founder, XPmedia
XPmedia.com
Maricopa, Arizona, United States

A Fork in the Road

MY hope and desire for you is that through this book you will get a strong biblical yet practical understanding that the supernatural life is for you to live and experience every day.

Your heavenly Father wants His supernatural Kingdom of love in demonstration to leak into your workplace, family, marriage, daily chores and duties, and whatever your full-time ministry may be. Reading this book could be, and hopefully will be, one of those spiritual milestones in your life that will set you on a new journey of discovery of the life you're called to live.

People quite often say to me, "Shawn, we hear your stories; we hear about the supernatural, and it's encouraging—and I want that—but I'm just not like you." Let me encourage you with this truth: living and walking in the supernatural has nothing to do with your personality but everything to do with Jesus on the inside of you and His eternal Kingdom where your citizenship lies (see Phil. 3:20).

Often when people hear words like *prophetic, healing,* and *supernatural,* they disqualify themselves. They think such things are only for the elite few who are chosen. Sure, some may have more predominant gifts than others, but one of the promises Jesus gave before He left the earth in the flesh was stated in John 14:12:

> *Most assuredly, I say to you, he who believes in Me, the works that I do he will do also; and greater works than these he will do, because I go to My Father.*

If we just believe in Him, we will do what He did and even greater things (or works) will we do because He went to the Father. He left us Holy Spirit to be the ultimate key holder to unlock all the secrets of the supernatural life. Holy Spirit's job description is to guide us into all truth. He is the tour guide for the experience of the Father's heavenly Kingdom while we're on this earth. He is not only our guarantee of the future promise (see Eph. 1:14), but also our Friend and Counselor.

To say these things are not for the average believer is to believe wrongly in the gospel message and finished work of the cross and to not fully understand the person and promise of Jesus Christ's work within the believer. We can access the impossible and the unimaginable not because of our own work or energy, but because of the power and energy that works within us (see Eph. 3:20).

I believe that to make the statement that the supernatural life is not for you is very unbiblical. God never called the qualified—He called the willing and the often seemingly unqualified. Look at Moses. He was considered the most humble leader in all of the land and could barely even speak. Yet, God chose him to lead a whole culture, an entire nation, out of Egypt and through the wilderness. God was so close to Moses that He spoke to him as a man would speak to a friend (see Ex. 33:11). God was not deterred by Moses' inabilities, insecurities, or failures. Moses' deficiencies were subject to God's power and grace, which always overrides any weakness of humanity.

Another response to whether the supernatural is for everyone is, "Well, I'm a little more timid, so I can only be used in the small group setting," or "She is more extroverted, so she would be great in a public setting." In the Kingdom life, often it is actually the opposite. Oftentimes God picks people who are the least likely, the most introverted, to get up on the stage. In the Kingdom, things work backwards— if you're quiet and timid, get ready because God's power will work through your weakness. If you're the loud extrovert, get ready because God also wants to use you but you cannot rely on your own strengths. You need to rely on Him who gives you strength and power.

Sometimes in settings where I'm ministering I hear things like, "It's easy for Shawn. He is loud, passionate, expressive, extroverted, and designed to be on the public platform." My response? That's only half the truth. Although part of my makeup is that I'm expressive and passionate, I was always a behind-the-scenes guy before I gave my heart to the Lord. I was, and still am, a drummer, and I despised being behind a mic in public. I quite enjoyed keeping to myself. I always said to myself that I would never be a public speaker—let alone in full-time vocational ministry. Ha! Little did I know how God would and could use me when I gave my heart to Him at 18 years of age. Never say never!

FALLING FORKS

During prayer about seven years ago, I went into a vision. I saw a swirling of angels in the room where I taught my "School of the Prophetic 101" at that time. These angelic beings began circling above, near the ceiling, creating what looked like a vortex. One definition of a vortex is a whirling mass of air in the form of a visible column or spiral—like a tornado.[1] The Lord then said to me, "I want you to go into that room"—the actual room I saw in my vision—"and lay down." So I went into the room and lay down. The moment I did, I went into the vision again and saw once again these angelic beings—this time they were dropping all these forks on the ground around me and beside me.

You may say, "Come on! Angels dropping forks? This is weird!" *Exactly!* It is very weird and abnormal, but we need to understand that all throughout the Bible when angels showed up, the things they did often weren't always "normal." The natural mind has a hard time understanding spiritual things. Hebrews 1:14 talks about how angels are ministering spirits sent to those who are heirs of salvation. Angelic ministry is part of my inheritance in and through Christ. They helped Jesus Christ throughout His ministry, so how much more will they help you and I now that we are united with Christ.

As these forks were being dropped on the ground all around me, I asked the Lord what He wanted to do and what He was saying to me through this vision. He began to speak to me about the fork in the road being given to the Body of Christ—of choosing between the North American normal of Christianity and the kind of Christianity that's actually lived out based upon the experiences laid out in the Bible.

For many of you, the message of this book can and will initiate in you a "fork in the road" experience.

I need to warn you that when you discover how easy it is and how called you are as a believer in Christ to live and experience the supernatural in your everyday life, it will destroy the boring, mundane mediocrity that has been fueled by religion and tradition and that robs you of the life promised in and through Christ through His finished work on the cross. Either you want to go all in, walking and growing into the fullness of the promises over you, or you just want to stay with what's comfortable, bound by a mindset of the fear of the unknown.

Jesus, as the head of His Body, the church, never had it in His heart for you just to attend good Sunday morning services and warm a pew or a squishy red, blue, or green contemporary church chair. His heart is for you to turn this world upside down with His supernatural gospel. Whether you're a conservative, Charismatic, Pentecostal, nondenominational, independent lone ranger, heresy hunter, or even a nonbeliever in the finished work of Jesus Christ, God's plan since the beginning was to transform you from the inside out and put His bloody stamp of righteousness on you. The end result? You will become like Christ and be conformed into the likeness and image of Him, the Son (see Rom. 8:29). You will fulfill all the destiny and promise over your life, living out of another dimension, just like Jesus said in John 18:36.

Through teaching on the supernatural and bringing awareness to the Body of Christ of their destiny and purpose, I have seen Holy Spirit put a fork in the road in many lives to shift their focus and everyday reality into a lifestyle of the supernatural. Just doing the Sunday thing and the nine-to-five, day-to-day living in survivor mode will not satisfy but will eventually bore you to spiritual dullness, if it hasn't already. Truly accessing the promises of God and growing into all that has been made available to you in Christ will completely satisfy. It's all about taking full advantage of what your union with Christ brings.

Ephesians 1:11 says, *"Furthermore, because we are united with Christ, we have received an inheritance from God..."* (NLT).

RAISING UP
PASSIONATE SONS OF GOD

God is raising up passionate sons and daughters who love Him and want to carry out Kingdom life on the earth. His plan and purpose for you come with enough grace and provision for you to fulfill everything He has called you to be and do, even if you feel you are not qualified.

It doesn't matter where you go to school or work; there is a grace for you to be a heavenly influence in your classroom and workplace. It may seem obvious to you where you are called to demonstrate His love and Kingdom, or you may be wondering how it would be possible for you to truly minister to your co-workers. You may wonder how you could actually minister and love people with a Jesus kind of love without being fired.

I promise you, God has not made a mistake. His heart for you was never to have you just go through the motions of life and work your job without representing Him in some way, shape, or form. You are not working at your job just to work at your job; there is a visible yet seemingly invisible purpose for you.

My wife, Michelle, made this amazing statement when she preached one night: "In the Kingdom we don't work for money; money works for us." This is a very biblically sound statement. If we are called to manifest the name of Jesus and make His Kingdom known and don't work for money, then what do we work for? Or we could ask ourselves, *Why am I really in the position I'm in, in life?* God said that we are to seek first His Kingdom and His righteousness and all the things we need will be given to us (see Matt. 6:33). In other words, provision for all our needs will follow as we keep His Kingdom in focus. The Kingdom must be first and everything else second.

Your Kingdom purpose must be first within the context of the reason why you are called to be wherever and whatever you are. You are not called to serve money; money is destined to serve you. Many people have the mentality, "I just work at my job to pay the bills." That is not God's plan for you; even if the season is temporary, there is still a Kingdom purpose behind what you are currently doing. God orders the steps of the righteous and is not surprised by any time, season, or situation in your life. It's all designed by Him, even if you are not in what some would call the perfect will of God for your life. God still has a plan for you in the middle of where you are right now.

Wherever you find yourself in life, God's heart for you is that the Word would become flesh, or made manifest in and through your life visibly. Just because you and I are declared righteous by Jesus does not mean we are living out that righteousness day to day. Romans 5:1 says that as a believer in Christ's finished work of the gospel, you are positionally righteous, but many don't understand this truth. Revelation of a truth should and will release freedom into your life, which then expresses itself in everything that you do (see John 8:32).

The Word, the *rhema* or *logos* of truth that comes from the Lord, is like a seed that goes into your spirit that carries life. Just as in the natural a seed grows and produces harvest through the right conditions and environment—rain, sunlight, good soil, etc.—so does the Word in you need to be nurtured and taken care of so you can manifest the Word in flesh form. You could argue and say, "Shawn, you're focusing too much on the external." I say, the reality is that the internal always affects the external. Your belief system, when it's a true belief, will always speak for itself in and through your life to those around you. You can talk all you want and have all the revelation and knowledge that you want, but if that revelation knowledge is not translating into your lifestyle in some way, I would highly question if that revelation is in your heart and you truly believe it.

We are called to be believers first, not just good scholars and theologians. The pharisaical mind worshiped the knowledge of the Word itself and totally missed Truth—Himself. We worship the living Word who is Jesus Christ, and Holy Spirit unveils the truth of the written Word so we can become like Jesus in function and expression (see John 1:14).

Remember, God is raising up sons and daughters to carry out His Kingdom on earth. When people look at these sons and daughters— at you—they should see Jesus because of your union with Him and because it's not a head knowledge-based religion but a new creation reality expressed in and through you (see 2 Cor. 5:17). His desire for you is that you would choose the road to a committed Kingdom life, not the road to mediocrity. This is the fork in the road, and Holy Spirit and the angels are committed to assisting you in this journey of unlocking the secrets of the supernatural life.

TESTIMONIES AND TIPS

I have purposely included many personal testimonies of the supernatural, not to bring attention to myself, but to encourage you with the experiential reality of Jesus for the everyday life of the believer. Cynics and critical people seem to always come down on sharing any kind of testimony, insinuating that it points back to the individual. My desire is that you would see the beauty and reality of Jesus Christ through everything shared. Let the testimonies whet your appetite for a greater expression of the supernatural Kingdom of God in your own life. You were created and destined for it.

I encourage you to meditate and study for yourself the Scriptures referenced throughout concerning the supernatural life. I have found that as I meditate on the Scriptures and write them out, I retain them, and then they are easily remembered. Something happens when Scripture goes into your eyes then out through your hands onto paper; it then hits your heart and is retained there. This is one of the ways I used to memorize the Word. I would rewrite Scripture on my computer for hours at a time and then often share what the Lord was speaking to me about Scripture with other people. As I did that, and rewrote and shared it, something began to happen inside as it became part of who I was.

I believe we need to share what we learn with others. This is a principle of stewardship and of the power of our testimony. We open ourselves up to access more of what's available to us as we give away what the Lord is doing in and through us (see 1 Cor. 4:2). I'm not saying we should throw all our pearls before the pigs (see Matt. 7:6) since we still need discernment and wisdom in what we say, when we say it, and who we say it to. But we do need to understand the heart of the Father in sharing what He is doing in and through our lives (see Gal. 6:6).

My prayer for you is that through this book, the supernatural in you will become normal and evident in your everyday life.

ENDNOTE

1. Dictionary.com. *Dictionary.com Unabridged,* s.v. "vortex," Random House, Inc., accessed February 28, 2012, http://dictionary.reference.com/browse/vortex.

CHAPTER I

Heaven on Earth Through You

Your kingdom come. Your will be done on earth as it is in heaven.
(Luke 11:2b)

WHEN searching for the secrets of the supernatural life, we must start with discovering and understanding the reality of the Kingdom of God. This is where every journey into the supernatural begins. We will thoroughly examine this vital key to unlocking the supernatural lifestyle that we are called to live.

First of all, let's define the word *kingdom*. Kingdom means "king's domain." It is the place in which the King of kings Himself lives and dwells. It is the place of His rule and reign and the domain of His supernatural power. As a believer in Christ who has full access to His

Kingdom, I am responsible to administrate that supernatural power when sharing the message of the gospel of Jesus Christ. Jesus' lifestyle was a daily demonstration of love and power with teaching. It's very easy for believers, even ministers, to become so intellectual in their faith that they come to a place where it's only about speaking a message, never about demonstrating God's power, and this is so sad. Paul said, in First Corinthians 2:4-5:

> *And my speech and my preaching were not with persuasive words of human wisdom, but in **demonstration of the Spirit and of power**, that your faith should not be in the wisdom of men but in the **power of God**.*

It doesn't matter who you are or what you do, as a believer of Christ, He has destined you to walk like He did. First John 2:6 says, *"He who says he abides in Him ought himself also to walk just as He walked."* Jesus said if we believe in Him, we will do what He did—and even greater things (see John 14:12).

This reality is an offense to many people who like everything packaged and professional and don't want what sometimes looks like chaos to take place in a church service or other type of meeting. In Acts 2 when Holy Spirit showed up on the Day of Pentecost, it looked chaotic to the average outsider in Jerusalem. The crowd that gathered accused the followers of Jesus of being drunk; they didn't understand the unexpected and disorderly things that seemed to be going on. Yet, in the midst of everything taking place, the first great harvest of souls came into the Kingdom. Three thousand people encountered the reality of Heaven that day and what seemed like "chaos" to those observing then has continued to increase ever since. This moment in time became the benchmark and standard for receiving a great harvest of souls. Genuine

Holy Ghost outpouring always ends in great harvest and transformation. People who are searching for spiritual truth and experience are hungry for the unknown and unexplained, for what sometimes seems out of the box. Lord, let what seems like chaos continue. If its source is You, we want it!

There is a wide chasm between those in the church who want cookie-cutter Christianity and those who want charismania. We need a balance of both. And we need to remember that one individual or one denomination does not have the 100-percent accurate perspective on how things should be. Ultimately, everyone is searching for *"the form of the Lord,"* just like Moses. And he was a man who saw the form (see Num. 12:8). I believe we can model a healthy balance that truly pushes Kingdom advancement in the church and in the culture.

This revelation of His Kingdom is so vital if we want to move into a lifestyle of supernatural encounter with Jesus; it's the very core of His message. First Corinthians 4:20 says, *"The Kingdom of God is not just a lot of talk; it is living by God's power"* (NLT), and we remember this truth especially in our ministry travels. Most of the time, we open our meetings with a demonstration of the Kingdom, whether it's prophetic words or words of knowledge for healing. When even one miracle pops open in a meeting, it has the potential to create a whole movement of faith in the room. When one kingdom is manifested, another kingdom has to go. That's why when demons manifest in our meetings, we know it's a sign that the Kingdom has come. Jesus said in Luke 11:20, *"If I cast out demons with the finger of God, surely the kingdom of God has come upon you."* In our meetings during worship, many times we have heard loud blood-curdling screams. As the Kingdom seems to become more tangible in the room, people start being delivered. No one prayed for them. The Kingdom was just revealed in a real, tangible way and the darkness had to leave. It's what I call a sovereign deliverance; we just create space for God to do what He wants to do and amazing things happen as a result.

> *So He said to them, "When you pray, say: Our Father in heaven, hallowed be Your name. Your kingdom come. Your will be done on earth as it is in heaven"* (Luke 11:2).

Based upon this scripture and others throughout the Bible, we know for certain that it is God's will for Heaven to invade every area of our lives. We need to begin to welcome into the atmosphere around us now the *"as it is in heaven"* experience whether it is through us or something else the Lord wants to do. Psalm 115:16 says, *"The heaven, even the heavens, are the Lord's; but the earth He has given to the children of men."* Jesus died so we would be reconciled to the Father through the removal of the dominion and wall of sin and spiritual isolation. Through this, He also gave us back the keys of authority to rule and reign with Him in this earth.

A NEW COVENANT PRAYER

John 3:3 says, *"Jesus answered and said to him, 'Most assuredly, I say to you, unless one is born again, he cannot see the kingdom of God.'"* When Jesus died on the cross, He did not just die for our sin and our healing, or just for the one day in the future when we receive our glorified body and live with Him for all eternity. That's the end result, yes. But He also died so that we can live an abundant life on the earth now. He paved the way for our invitation into a Kingdom encounter or a Kingdom life on the earth now. Jesus' prayer for His disciples in Luke 11:2 was that His Kingdom would come on earth as it is in Heaven, here and now. His prayer was acknowledging that life on earth wasn't the way it could or should be, and that this prayer needed to be their hearts' cry.

Jesus outlined this prayer before establishing the New Covenant, but it still needs to be on our lips and needs to be a desire in every believer. However, we can tweak it a bit, as follows: *God, now that I am seated in heavenly places and that being my place of citizenship, help me release Your Kingdom on earth as it is in Heaven now. If I am seated with Him and if I am declared righteous and have the authority and power of Christ in me, then I become a gateway for Heaven on the earth. So, God, let Heaven invade earth through everything that I do and say.* This shifts the focus from just waiting on God to do a sovereign Kingdom work, to us (who have been given an inheritance) to take action and administrate the Kingdom here and now. That should be the goal of every believer, to live Heaven on earth now in his or her experience of life. We can say all the right things and believe the right theology about the Kingdom, but it needs to be a tangible, visible experience in our everyday life.

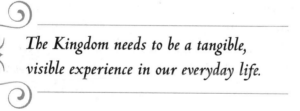

The Kingdom needs to be a tangible, visible experience in our everyday life.

The born-again, new creation experience is not just a ticket to Heaven just in case the end of the world comes tomorrow. Many look at salvation as a ticket to a way out of this world, waiting for the sweet by-and-by to pick them up and save them from suffering. John 10:10 says He came to give us life and life abundant—not only in Heaven one day but also on the earth in this temporary life here and now! Let's accept it, believe it, and live it. Your body will die at some point, and you will leave this earth (and eventually return to a new Heaven and new earth here with your glorified, resurrected body). However, God is inviting you into this experience of Heaven on earth *now*.

Many people pray the prayer in Luke 11, which many refer to as the Lord's prayer. It is not a prayer that the Lord would pray, however, because part of it would not apply to Him. The New Living Translation of Luke 11:4 says, *"and forgive us our sins...."* He had no sin to be forgiven of. It was a prayer in that time for the disciples to pray. Now, as New Covenant believers, contrary to popular belief, we don't confess our sins to be forgiven. We confess our sins because we were forgiven before we ever even sinned! Jesus forgave us over 2,000 years ago before we were born (see 1 Pet. 3:18). So after our initial salvation experience, we now confess our sins, not to be forgiven—which devalues the forgiveness He paid for on the cross—but to come into agreement with what has already been done. By His grace, forgiveness has been made available because He has paid for our sin.

Please don't get me wrong, we still need to repent and confess to the Lord. Repentance, though, is simply a changing of perspective and confession is an acknowledgment of the sufficient grace that has been made available in Christ by admitting our weaknesses and failures. I think we place too much emphasis on penance and trying to convince God to forgive us when He already did and has. If believers are still confessing sins of the past that have already been dealt with, then that explains the cloud of condemnation that seems to linger around people all the time. There is no condemnation in Christ (see Rom. 8:1). There is freedom in the truth of the finished work of the cross of Christ. You can't dig up your old nature because it is dead and has been buried with Christ once you accepted Him into your life as Lord (see Rom. 6:4-8). The devil will trick you into believing that you have dug up your old self and need to work at killing it. This notion is what condemnation feeds on. Right believing in the finished work of the cross of Jesus Christ will always be what sets us free experientially.

BORN OF HEAVEN

The born-again experience is the initiation into a lifestyle of the Kingdom of God in and through a person's life on the earth. It is the very reality that has positioned us in two places at once. In John 3:13, we see Jesus saying to Nicodemus, *"No one has ascended to heaven but He who came down from heaven, that is, the Son of Man who is in heaven."* In this pre-cross statement, Jesus was setting the new standard that would one day apply to all those who would be born again. Those who become born from above (see John 3:3) would have two homes: their eternal and their temporal. Jesus was saying that although He came down from Heaven and dwelt on the earth, in that moment He was also in Heaven. Do you know why you were destined to experience Heaven on earth? It's because you have been raised with Christ and are seated with Him in heavenly places (see Eph. 2:6). Heaven is our eternal home and it gives God good pleasure to show us around our home. In Heaven there is no sickness, no disease, no sorrow, no depression, no death, no poverty—nothing that has come as a result of sin entering the world. Heaven is health, prosperity, and wholeness. It's not just God, but also all of His stuff—power, angels, living creatures—everything described in the Book of Revelation. Things that are inexpressible are found in this place. Paul, in Second Corinthians 12:2-4, went up to the third heaven, and there he had a wild heavenly encounter. He said, *"...whether in the body I do not know, or whether out of the body I do not know, God knows—such a one was caught up to the third heaven. And I know such a man—whether in the body* or out of the body I do not know, God knows—how he was caught up into Paradise and heard inexpressible words, which it is not lawful for a man to utter." Much of what Paul saw could not be described through earthly language. I've had encounters with God and seen things that I still have a hard time describing. Sometimes heavenly experiences can seem like a weird sci-fi movie.

HIS WILL?

People say, "Well, what is the will of God for my life? I don't understand what He wants for my life." The will of God is simply Heaven on earth in every area of your life—Heaven on earth in your family, finances, job, community, ministry, and your street. That's the will of God for your life. When you can live according to that under-standing, life will become less complicated. You won't be chasing after a calling, a title, or some platform of influence and ministry. You can search and search and never find what you think is His will for you, while the whole time His will has been right in front of you and so simple. It is Heaven on earth for you—now. Ask yourself, *Is Heaven invading earth in my life right now? Am I allowing Heaven to invade my workplace? My home?* That's the will of God for you. God is taking you out of the attic of isolation from this truth and reality, and is dusting you off with His holy feather duster.

> *The will of God is simply Heaven on earth in every area of your life.*

Dust gathers easily when things are not moving. Not having a revelation of His Kingdom invading our lives now, is like putting ourselves into a spiritual attic of isolation. Swamps are swamps because of stagnant water. But Jesus said if we believe, out of our bellies will flow rivers of living water. This is the inheritance call of believers; we are to let our lights shine and let the rivers of life flow from within us. These rivers are the life-giving waters from the very throne of God in Heaven. It's the power of Christ in believers to advance His Kingdom on earth.

> *. . .Jesus stood and cried out, saying, "If anyone thirsts, let him come to Me and drink. He who believes in Me, as the Scripture has said, out of his heart will flow rivers of living water"* (John 7:37-38).

God wants to come to you today to wipe off all the religious swampy grime that has been an influencing residue on your life because you never really understood the true message of the Kingdom and its place in your everyday life and experience. It's a lot harder for dust to stick to something when it's constantly moving; the Kingdom in us is destined to move in and through us every day. When you feel dull in your spiritual life, it is usually first and foremost the busyness of life that has replaced quality time and communication with the Lord. Second, you may have dammed up the life inside by being a spiritual hoarder. We are commissioned to freely give what God has given us (see Matt. 10:8). Those rivers need to be moving. Dullness is exactly what a swamp feels like— there is no movement.

THE KINGDOM
IS NOT OF THIS WORLD

In John 18:36 Jesus said, *"My kingdom is not of this world."* It is not of this cosmos, not of this earthly order. He was saying that His Kingdom is of a different order, a different government, a different dimension. It's the government of Heaven. That is the government that He ruled from—from the heavenly realm to this earthly realm. He received His orders from there, not here.

Jesus was actually speaking this to Pilate in a place where they made governmental decisions. He told Pilate that if His Kingdom were of this world, His servants would have fought and He wouldn't have been delivered to the Jews. He said He would have been protected. Jesus was basically saying that it was God who sanctioned what happened to Him on earth. No one but God had any control over Him. He was an ambassador, a representation and the full expression of the heavenly Father. When you encounter the Kingdom on the earth, you're not encountering an earthly dimension. You're encountering a supernatural dimension of God: His Kingdom.

I visited Moravian Falls in North Carolina many years ago because I had heard many amazing reports about angelic encounters that were taking place. The Moravians were a group of radical young missionaries who settled in North Carolina in 1752 and were said to be known for their 24-hour prayer initiatives. It was said that they prayed there for 100 years, 24 hours a day.[1] As a result, many believed there was this amazing awareness of heavenly realities and the angelic realm in that area. I had heard some pretty wild testimonies from different prophets and others who had visited Moravian Falls. I was instructed to go to where many of these encounters were supposed to have happened—a place called Prayer Mountain.

I was open to what I might encounter there, and I won't go into all the details, but let me just say I had a life-changing experience. I found a pathway leading up to Prayer Mountain, which was more like a small hill. As soon as I stepped onto the cement pathway that led up the hill, I had an open vision. I saw what looked like a giant, ancient gate that opened up over me and made a loud creak as it swung open. I walked through the gate and it seemed as if I had walked into a scene right from C.S. Lewis' *The Chronicles of Narnia*. It felt like a whole other dimension. I walked into another world. I knew something big was going to happen and, to make a long story short, I had a 45-minute angelic encounter that changed my life. This experience marked the official launch of our ministry. It was amazing. That's what happens when you encounter the other world of the Kingdom. The Kingdom of God is of another dimension, truly another world, and is not like the world we temporarily live in.

Some people say they want God, but not all of the "weird, super-natural stuff." The Bible says in Matthew 6:33, *"Seek first the kingdom."* No one can separate the King from His Kingdom. No one can separate Him from where He lives. The most important part of the Kingdom is the gospel of Jesus Christ and who He is. Jesus is the doorway to the Kingdom. Matthew 11:4 says, *"Jesus answered and said to them, 'Go and tell John the things which you hear and see.'"* As I said earlier, the Kingdom message is not just what you hear but also what you see demonstrated. This message of the gospel of the Kingdom of God that Jesus came declaring, started with "Repent!" Change your perspective because a new law has come to town. The new law was the Spirit of life that came to fulfill the law of sin and death that man could not fulfill. Jesus came with a controversial message, one that the religious couldn't understand and even rejected because of the donkey-riding package it came in. He didn't just have a message; He was the message and He manifested the realities of the message—Heaven on earth. He demonstrated the Kingdom in love, power, signs, and wonders.

You cannot live a supernatural life and share or preach the gospel in its full effect if you don't demonstrate the Kingdom. The full gospel message is salvation, healing, deliverance, raising the dead, cleansing the leper, loving the orphans, loving the widows, taking care of the hungry, and the like—that's the full gospel. You can't separate them. Some people say, "Well, I like the salvation part." Or "I like the healing part," or "I like helping orphans," or "I like helping to feed the hungry." Many pick and choose, but these things are all parts of the same package.

It is too easy to say, "Well, I have a healing ministry," "I have a deliverance ministry," "I have a salvation ministry," "I have a feeding the hungry ministry," or "I have a homeless ministry," but Jesus came for the whole person—the practical *and* the spiritual. Believers need to have a *Jesus ministry.* He said to John's disciples in Matthew 11:4-5:

> *Go and tell John the things which you **hear and see:** The blind see and the lame walk; the lepers are cleansed and the deaf hear; the dead are raised up and the poor have the gospel preached to them.*

Matthew 9:35 says:

> *Jesus went about all the cities and villages, teaching in their synagogues, preaching the gospel of the kingdom, and healing every sickness and every disease among the people.*

At another place Jesus said:

> *Whatever city you enter, and they receive you, eat such things as are set before you. And* **heal the sick there**, *and say to them,* **"The kingdom of God has come near** *to you"* (Luke 10:8-9).

Why would Jesus say to heal the sick there and then say the Kingdom of God has come near? It is because when the sick are healed, it is a sign that the Kingdom of God has come near. When the Kingdom comes, demons leave, sickness has to go, healing happens. So He is saying, when you go there, heal the sick there. Do the demonstration of the Kingdom and then declare to them that the Kingdom has come near to them. This is part of the fruit of the full gospel message of Jesus Christ. Romans 15:18-19 says:

> *For I will not dare to speak of any of those things which Christ has not accomplished through me, in word and deed, to make the Gentiles obedient—in* **mighty signs and wonders, by the power of the Spirit of God**, *so that from Jerusalem and round about to Illyricum* **I have fully preached the gospel of Christ**.

While I was ministering in a meeting one time, a very powerful atmosphere of healing came over the whole place. People were being healed of all sorts of ailments. There was a young woman in the foyer, and somebody grabbed me and asked me to go pray for her. As I began praying for her, I could sense some witchcraft and discerned that she was dabbling in some spiritual mixture. She had a belief in Jesus, but He was not Lord in her life. I asked God what He wanted to do because often God will give us a key to unlock the miracle or unlock the door for someone to receive a miracle.

As I began to pray into some specific things, I felt the Lord show me that something had broken off of her. One of the men who had traveled with me on this trip was standing about 15 feet away, and all of sudden he said he saw in the spirit a spider jump out of her head and scurry out of the building. I knew immediately that something demonic had broken off of her life. The interesting thing was that she had just purchased a new pair of prescription glasses and was considered legally blind without them. They were quite expensive, said the man who asked me to pray for her. One week later, I received word that her eyes were completely healed and she didn't need glasses to see anymore. The Kingdom was released with deliverance and healing power, and the greater Kingdom drove out the lesser.

RAISING THE DEAD

I was thinking one day that we needed to start raising the dead as Jesus said in His commission to His disciples.

> And as you go, preach, saying, "The kingdom of heaven is at hand."
> Heal the sick, cleanse the lepers, **raise the dead,** cast out demons.
> Freely you have received, freely give (Matthew 10:7-8).

As a disciple of Jesus today, you are destined for these experiences in your life as well. Just because you may not be in a pulpit preaching Sunday to Sunday or traveling in an itinerant ministry doesn't exclude you from this mandate in your life.

To raise the dead, we need to go where the dead are. You're probably thinking, *What!? Are you kidding?* It is the same as going to where the sick are if we want to see them healed. Most of the dead are in hospital morgues or in funeral homes prior to burial. Now, I'm not at all sanctioning going to graveyards and lying on graves trying to raise corpses from the ground—although that did happen after Jesus gave up His spirit on the cross and was resurrected; dead people did come out of their graves (see Matt. 27:52-53). Imagine if that happened at your local cemetery one Sunday. Wow!

I believe the church should be the first place that people bring their dead, just as they would the sick and oppressed. We need to start positioning our churches in North America to raise the dead. So how do we do that? Well, since they aren't being brought to us, we've got to go to them. I'm not talking about spiritually dead. We deal with that all of the time. I'm talking about the physically dead.

One night during a local meeting I was leading, I felt inspired to take a first step. We were already doing weekly outreach, so we decided we were going to do our first raise-the-dead outreach. Remember, this was part of the gospel message (see Matt. 10:5-8; 11:4-6). We went to the hospital and found out through a series of events where the morgue room was. The door was actually unlocked, to my surprise. We didn't go in as I probably would have been arrested, but we did spend about three hours in the hospital praying for the dead to come alive. First, we put our hands on the morgue door, then moved to the stairwell across from the room, then ended up in the hospital multi-faith prayer room down the hallway. We did not see the dead raised, but we sowed a seed of faith to see the raising of the dead through prayer.

I believe God saw our hearts of faith and liked what He saw. We had a few trying to warn us away from this and tell us that we shouldn't do it, but here's the thing—what do we have to lose by stepping out and believing the Word of God? I know that a couple resurrections from the dead would change everything in a community, city, region, and beyond. Sure, maybe after the first resurrection some influential scientist, doctor, or media reporter would present some ridiculous explanation to bring it down to an earthly level of possibility, but after two or three there would be no question in people's minds and hearts that a greater Force was behind it all. We have to think bigger than our church culture—we have to think Kingdom culture, and our blueprint is found in Scripture and based on our relationship with God Almighty.

> *We have to think bigger than our church culture—*
> *we have to think Kingdom culture!*

WHERE IS THE KINGDOM OF GOD?

Where is the Kingdom of God? According to Matthew 10:7, the Kingdom is *"at hand."* At that time, Jesus was the representation of the Kingdom. He was the doorway to the Kingdom. *"At hand"* means within our grasp, all around, near, available to experience. The Kingdom is closer than many think. It is not some far-off, inaccessible, unapproachable realm.

During a meeting one time as I was ministering, I could feel a major change in the atmosphere. Then God gave me some words of knowledge—one specific word about a deaf left ear. A few people responded, but before I could even pray, the worship leader up on stage put his hand up motioning that it was him who had the deaf ear. The moment I pointed at him, he felt a pop and then a hiss go through his left ear. When he came down off the stage for ministry, before I could pray for him, he realized that he was totally healed. He had had no eardrum since he was around five years of age—yet in one Kingdom moment, he was totally healed. God performed an incredible miracle.

When the at-hand experience of the Kingdom is recognized, anything can happen. We have been in meetings where people had to take out their hearing aids because in that atmosphere they were completely healed. At times people have screamed out, "I can hear! I can hear!" That happens because God loves people.

> *So that they brought the sick out into the streets and laid them on beds and couches, that at least the shadow of Peter passing by might fall on some of them* (Acts 5:15).

In this scripture, we see that Peter carried an atmosphere of the Kingdom and people were healed and delivered because of it. We can release the Kingdom by the spoken word, but the Kingdom can also manifest in the atmosphere around us like Peter experienced. Holy Spirit overshadowed Peter just like He did Mary at the conception of Jesus. Luke 1:35 says, *"And the angel answered and said to her, 'The Holy Spirit will come upon you, and the power of the Highest will overshadow you; therefore, also, that Holy One who is to be born will be called the Son of God.'"*

There have been times when we were ministering on the street that, when people got around the atmosphere, they were drawn into an encounter with Jesus. One time I was in Mexico, and a few of us were outside ministering on the street, praying for the sick. We were planning on eventually trying to get into the hospital to pray for people. As we were walking toward the hospital and got close to the doors, a man called out, "I want to know Jesus!" Just out of nowhere. We weren't even talking to him, but something was tugging on his spirit. We prayed for the man, he received Jesus, and he was totally healed. It was amazing. When Jesus was here on the earth in the flesh, the Kingdom was at hand because He was the doorway standing wide open. Now that He lives within us, for those all around us the Kingdom is still at hand because we have become the administrators of the Kingdom. So the Kingdom of God is at hand—but also within you. Luke 17:21b says, *"The kingdom of God is within you."*

RELEASING THE KINGDOM FROM WITHIN

We have the ability to release the Kingdom from within us. Mark 4:35-41 is the story of Jesus in the storm with His disciples. Jesus was in the boat, lying down, sleeping on a pillow in the bow of the boat—in the middle of a very intense storm. The waves were crashing into the boat onto Jesus, filling the boat with water. The disciples were trained, seasoned, normally fearless fishermen. They had been through many storms before, but this one was different. Meanwhile their Leader continued snoring on a pillow. They eventually woke Him up, saying, "Jesus, don't You care that we are perishing?" The first thing Jesus did was look at the storm and say, *"Peace, be still."* He didn't address whether or not He cared that they were fearful until after, saying in verse 40, *"Why are you so fearful? How is it that you have no faith?"* Their unbelief is what created a place for fear, and God is always looking for faith. When He said, *"Peace, be still,"* He released the Kingdom from within, with His spoken word. His word created a platform and/or conduit for the Kingdom to be established. What He was doing in that moment was modeling what it's like to live a Kingdom life on the earth. In Heaven there are no storms. We can live in perfect peace, even in the midst of the greatest storm in our life, when we're operating from a Kingdom perspective. He was trying to model something for

His kids, for His students. He was hoping they would notice that if their Master was sleeping, the One who said in the beginning, "Let's cross over," then they would survive and really had no reason to fear. He wanted them to realize that they themselves could have calmed the storm because of the authority that they had been given. As children of God, we must learn how to release the Kingdom of Heaven through the spoken word, changing the very elements around us in our circumstances and situations.

MIRACLES, SIGNS, AND WONDERS

Understanding the message that the Kingdom of God is within you is the pathway to miracles, signs, and wonders. Acts 2:22 says:

> *Men of Israel, hear these words: Jesus of Nazareth, a Man attested by God to you by miracles, wonders, and signs which God did through Him in your midst, as you yourselves also know.*

We don't search for the sign—
the sign searches for faith.

Signs and wonders marked the ministry of Jesus, a man approved of the Father by the mighty miracles, signs, and wonders He did. We don't search for the sign—the sign searches for faith. Signs and wonders follow those who believe. Nicodemus, a Pharisee, was speaking to Jesus in the following verse, *"This man came to Jesus by night and said to Him, 'Rabbi, we know that You are a teacher come from God; for no one can do these signs that You do unless God is with him'"* (John 3:2). First Thessalonians 1:5 says, *"For our gospel did not come to you in word only, but also in power, and in the Holy Spirit and in much assurance...."* The power of Heaven backs up faith and the message of the gospel of love and grace. I especially love not only when we see supernatural signs in our meetings, but also when we see them out in the restaurants, in the malls, and on the streets. Every time signs and wonders have been revealed, people have had encounters with Jesus in such powerful ways. We need to see the value of supernatural signs and wonders, but we need most of all to keep our eyes on Jesus.

SEEING INTO THE UNSEEN
(HAVING KINGDOM EYES)

It is God's heart that we begin to see with eyes of the Kingdom in our everyday life. Second Corinthians 4:18 says, *"...we fix our gaze on things that cannot be seen. For the things we see now will soon be gone, but the things we cannot see will last forever"* (NLT). The unseen reality around us is more real than the seen in front of us. The seen was actually made out of what is unseen (see Heb. 11:3).

In John 4:35, Jesus is talking to His disciples and says:

> Do you not say, *"There are still four months and then comes the harvest"?* Behold, I say to you, lift up your eyes and look at the fields, for they are already white for harvest!

In other words, open your eyes to see beyond the natural and into the invisible, eternal reality. Yes, there is a season for harvest in the natural and even a process of time for that harvest—but I want you to look beyond what your mind can understand and see into the invisible.

If we can learn to see beyond our natural circumstances and into the spiritual realm, there will be more of a manifestation of the Kingdom in our lives. We have to learn to see with eyes of the Kingdom. Mark 6:30-44 recounts the story of Jesus' feeding more than 5,000 people with only a few loaves and a few fishes—it is the perfect example of seeing a situation with Kingdom eyes.

Jesus and His disciples got into a boat to go away and rest awhile. But when they reached their destination, a multitude of people met them. Jesus chose to teach them, and after a long day, the disciples wanted to send the people away so they could find something to eat. The fact that the people would have had to be told to leave is quite interesting. Clearly, the great spiritual hunger within them superseded their natural hunger. They didn't even think of leaving to feed themselves. They were encountering the True Living Manna from Heaven. The Bread of Life Himself was imparting nourishment to them. Jesus' response to the disciples' counsel to send the people away to eat was this:

> But He answered and said to them, **"You give them something to eat."** And they said to Him, "Shall we go and buy two hundred denarii worth of bread and give them something to eat?" But He said to them, **"How many loaves do you have? Go and see."** And when they found out they said, "Five, and two fish" (Mark 6:37-38).

There are three interesting facts—which I highlighted—to look at in this passage of scripture. *Number one*, Jesus said to them, "*You give them something to eat,"* suggesting that they could do it themselves. The disciples immediately rationalized the situation and again looking through their intellect, thought maybe He meant for them to go into town and buy some bread for the people. *Number two,* He said to them, *"How many loaves do you have?"* Once again Jesus seems to be suggesting that it's possible to feed the crowd even though in the natural He and they both knew they had not brought with them a boat full of food to feed 5,000 people. In their minds the disciples were probably thinking, *Jesus, we all came in the same boat together. You know we don't have enough loaves, so why are You even asking us this question?* You see, Jesus was trying to encourage and motivate Kingdom sight in the disciples in that very moment. He wanted them to see based upon faith in the nature of God El Shaddai, the all-sufficient One, the God of abundance—but they still were not getting it.

Then, *number three,* Jesus finally says, *"Go and see."* Now He's gone too far, the disciples were probably thinking. *What is the point? We know we don't have enough food to feed all these people.* It was a ridiculous request to them. But this was "Mentoring 101" for the disciples and they were missing it totally. It is elementary faith to believe that Jesus is the Provider, the God of more than enough. We can't base what we do or don't do on what we see or don't see. Jesus was trying to get the disciples to see beyond their natural circumstances and into the unseen realm, simply by revelation of who He is. In the Kingdom realm, there is always more than enough. Jesus was basically saying to His disciples, "Listen, guys, go and see with Kingdom eyes that in the few loaves you have there are many, many other loaves—enough to feed all these hungry people in front of you." Recently God spoke a riddle to me, saying, "Shawn, a seed is not a tree and a tree is not a seed, but it is." He then began to explain to me that in that one seed is a tree and in that tree is many, many more seeds, which then produces many, many more trees and so on. When we look at the little that we have, we need to see with eyes of the Kingdom motivated through faith.

A seed can be likened to anything that has the potential to multiply and produce fruit. It can be your talents, skills, gifts, time, or finances. In your wallet you may see $50, but God sees way more than just $50. He sees the potential of that $50 seed because of the DNA of multiplication within that $50, if used correctly. He sees that $50 seed as a tree with thousands of more seeds connected to it. Remember, in the Kingdom there is always more than enough. We must learn to see what God sees. What Jesus was saying when He said, *"Go and see,"* was, "I want you to see the potential in the little that you have. If you can utilize and steward the little that you have, more will be given to you, and you'll activate a miracle, drawing on My supernatural manifestation of abundance and provision." To access the miraculous, we need to see beyond the natural circumstances around us. We begin to see into that unseen Kingdom realm of abundant provision by revelation of who Jesus is. When we operate and see by faith through the truth of who Jesus says He is, we access miraculous provision for the need.

Seeing is the first step, but then we must follow up quickly by stepping out and acting, based upon what we have seen in the unseen. It wasn't until the disciples took what they had and began to pass it out that the loaves and fish began to multiply, thereby accessing the miraculous.

RIGHTEOUSNESS, PEACE, AND JOY

Paul said in Romans 14:17, *"The kingdom of God is not eating and drinking, but righteousness and peace and joy in the Holy Spirit."* Righteousness is always partnered with the Kingdom. We can't separate the two. Righteousness and justice are the foundation of His throne in Heaven (see

Ps. 97:2; 89:14). People want Kingdom power without character; they want to be righteous positionally but not live out that righteousness. I remember years ago when I first launched into full-time ministry and was going through a tough test, predominantly with the church I was attending. My character was being stretched to grow, and my integrity was being established. During this season, someone spoke a word of wisdom to me to encourage me. He said, "Shawn, the gift is like the tip of an iceberg. Everyone loves looking at it and is wowed by it, but what they don't see is how deep the iceberg goes beneath the water, and that's the character and integrity for the calling of God over your life. That's what is being built right now." This word of wisdom brought clarity and strength for me in that season, allowing me to pass the tests that surrounded me.

The Kingdom is also about peace and *joy* in and through Holy Spirit. Joy stems from the peace with God that we have (see Rom. 5:1), born from our right standing with Him. You should have fun in your spiritual life. Laughter is good. You'd be surprised how many people believe more in being serious and stoic in church than in being full of joy. A lot of people don't like laughing and wonder, "Why is she laughing in church? Why can't he control his laughter?" Too many people think that God is not fun, that He is boring. But I'm here to tell you that He wants you to laugh. In fact, God laughs. Psalm 2:4a says, *"He who sits in the heavens shall laugh."* He invented laughter; you can only laugh because He gave you the ability to laugh. There is no joy in hell. There's only joy in Heaven. In fact, there's fullness of joy in the presence of God. The Bible says, *"A merry heart* [laughter] *does good, like medicine"* (Prov. 17:22a). When speaking of giving, Second Corinthians 9:7 says, *"So let each one give as he purposes in his heart, not grudgingly or of necessity; for God loves a cheerful giver."* The word *cheerful* is *hilaros* in the Greek, describing a spirit of enjoyment that sweeps away all restraints, compared to being under the restraint and bondage of giving grudgingly.

The English transliteration of this word *hilaros* is *hilarious.*[2] God desires hilarious joy to sweep over us in giving. Could this be the pathway to the abounding grace of supply that is promised in the next verse? Joy is always coupled with faith, whereas doing things out of necessity and grudgingly is not. *"And God is able to make all grace abound toward you, that you, always having all sufficiency in all things, may have an abundance for every good work"* (2 Cor. 9:8). Joy is a fruit of faith as it is of the Spirit. David's heart cry in Psalm 51:12 was, *"Restore to me the joy of Your salvation, and uphold me by Your generous Spirit."* Our salvation is the starting point for joy, and in the presence of God there is fullness of joy (see Ps. 16:11). Why? It is because in His presence there is no room for the restraint of bondage, for doing things grudgingly or in unbelief. Joy in our life is a direct result of a right perspective of who God is, and in this place we declare that God is good by our actions—thus enabling us to receive the abounding grace and abundance of provision for every good work. So go from doing things out of religious obligation and restraint to allowing His joy to permeate your every decision, and watch what begins to happen.

THE KEYS

In Matthew 16:19, Jesus says to Peter, *"I will give you the keys of the kingdom of heaven, and whatever you bind on earth will be bound in heaven, and whatever you loose on earth will be loosed in heaven."* This literally means that whatever has been released on earth has already been released in Heaven and that whatever has been bound on earth has already been bound in Heaven. Having the keys of the Kingdom means having the keys to the unseen realm. Keys open doors and a different key is needed for every door. This can be likened to having the method for unlocking the breakthrough in a situation or circumstance that one faces. Jesus modeled this to His disciples; He constantly changed His methods for releasing the Kingdom on earth as He received directives from the Father. To release Heaven on earth, we must follow the leading of God just like Jesus did (see John 5:19). He only did what He saw His Father doing in heavenly places. He took direction from the top.

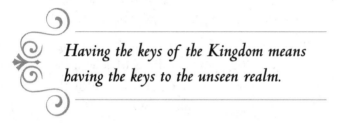

Having the keys of the Kingdom means having the keys to the unseen realm.

As I just noted, the keys of the Kingdom can be defined as the methods and actions of Heaven carried out on earth to release the Kingdom. There is a different key for different situations. We know the Source is always Jesus Christ, but the way we access a miracle may be unlocked through different Heaven-inspired methods. We need to know what the Lord wants to do in every situation and how He wants to do it. There are six recorded accounts of blind eyes being healed in Jesus' ministry. Three are different and not repeated in other Gospels:

1. Faith alone. *"Then Jesus said to him, 'Go your way; your faith has made you well.' And immediately he received his sight and followed Jesus on the road"* (Mark 10:52).

2. Spitting in the mud. *"When He had said these things, He spat on the ground and made clay with the saliva; and He anointed the eyes of the blind man with the clay"* (John 9:6). Jesus spat in the mud, and it was the key that unlocked the miracle.

3. Praying twice. *"So He took the blind man by the hand and led him out of the town. And when He had spit on his eyes and put His hands on him, He asked him if he saw anything. And he looked up and said, 'I see men like trees, walking.' Then He put His hands on his eyes again and made him look up. And he was restored and saw everyone clearly"* (Mark 8:23-25). Even Jesus prayed twice—how much more should we? Everything Jesus did was a model for us. If Jesus did it, we should follow His example. You may say He didn't actually pray. We have to change our grid and/or our understanding of what prayer is. Prayer is not always just getting down on my knees by my bed and putting my hands together, or even closing my eyes and talking to God. Prayer is demonstrated in many forms. In this passage, His actions were a prayer. Jesus was the very epitome of prayer; He embodied the very nature of a true man of prayer. If prayer is simply communication with the Father, He was communicating through His actions and a powerful miracle was released. In this case the miracle didn't happen the first time, but the second.

So we see the same miracle take place by three different methods, using three different keys. God told His prophet to tell Naaman to dip in the Jordan seven times (see 2 Kings 5:10). The Jordan was a very dirty river; it didn't make much sense that Naaman could be healed of the unclean disease of leprosy by washing in an unclean river. But this was the method of the Kingdom that brought the miracle. Remember when Elijah lay on the dead boy mouth to mouth, face to face to raise him from the dead? (See First Kings 17:19-23.) Such an unusual method, but it worked.

Weird things were done in the Bible to unlock the miraculous. Miracles don't always happen in the "I lay my hands on you and pray the prayer of faith" type of method. Although that is an amazing way to release the power of Heaven, sometimes God may tell you to release the word He's giving you and it will release the miracle. Sometimes God may say, "Just worship, and the miracle will happen."

I was in a meeting in Arizona, ministering, when something amazing took place. God moved powerfully. As I was walking back and forth in the front waiting for more direction from the Lord, all of a sudden I heard Holy Spirit say to me, "Hamburger." I said, "What?" He said, "The word *hamburger* means something to somebody. Just release the word." I was thinking, *You've got to be kidding.* But I understand that when you loose on earth what has been already loosed in Heaven, something significant on earth always takes place.

Remember, God's words don't return to Him void (see Isa. 55:11). So I released the word. I said it three times: "Hamburger. Hamburger. Hamburger." And every time, everybody laughed. Nothing happened, so I just had to move on trusting in Holy Spirit. I began to talk about alignment and what the Lord was doing in the Body of Christ. In about 15 minutes, this guy stood up to testify about a healing that he had just had while I was speaking. Over four years prior, he had a football accident—someone rammed into one of his knees. Since then, he had a problem bending his knee without pain. He stood up totally healed as his knee came into total alignment.

At the end of the meeting, he shared with me a dream that he had had a week earlier. In the dream, he was with some friends and they were all deciding on a specific code word that, when spoken, would bring his life into alignment both spiritually and physically. The friends suggested the code word *macaroni.* So when that word was spoken, all this alignment would take place in his life. He said, "Shawn, I didn't want the code word to be macaroni, so I said to my friends in the dream, I want the code word to be *hamburger* so when the word *hamburger* is spoken, my life would come into total alignment both spiritually and physically." Wow. I was floored and amazed by the goodness of God. *Hamburger* was spoken and the healing was released. Heaven and earth were synchronized at that very moment for that young man. When you release what you hear from Holy Spirit the way He tells you to, you unlock a manifestation of the Kingdom into the atmosphere and over an individual. The young man emailed me about a week later to explain all the positive things that had happened in his life since that word.

Matthew 11:12 says, *"...the kingdom of heaven suffers violence, and the violent take it by force."* That word for "violent" in the Greek means energetic[3]; the energetic ones will access the realities available to them in the Kingdom. Faith is not a passive, stagnant thing; rather, it is an energized, flowing, moving reality. We need to have an energized faith for Kingdom work. Choosing to believe is a choice you must make every day—even if you don't feel like it. I believe because of His grace gift of faith given to us, we don't have to feel faith to live from that truth and reality. We must continue every day to believe in who Jesus says He is. If God has given you a vision in business and you make mistakes, make bad deals, or fail at a particular venture, you still are called to keep on going. You must learn from your mistakes and keep on going. It's no different in the Kingdom.

When we were planning a ministry trip to Haiti in 2010, I told the organizer who would be helping facilitate our trip to make sure we had a sound system on hand with us and asked her to take us into the most voodoo-steeped village. I felt the need to set up speakers, demonstrate the miraculous, and then preach the gospel. When we arrived at this particular place, there were three high-level voodoo priests there. After we set up the sound system, I talked about the Kingdom, invited the crippled, deaf, and the sick, and declared that Jesus would heal them because of His love and power.

It was slow going at first. No one was responding. Eventually people starting coming, and miracles began to take place. After a few notable miracles had occurred, I preached the gospel message of Jesus Christ, and many people got saved. Not only did those who were in front of me get saved, but so did people in their huts who weren't even out on the street. It was amazing to see the miracles that took place, and Jesus made His name known. People renounced their voodoo and were healed.

ROADBLOCKS TO RIGHT BELIEVING AND THINKING

Unfortunately, there are roadblocks that keep the church from experiencing a greater manifestation of God's Kingdom on earth. Luke 11:52 speaks of Jesus rebuking the religious teachers of the law, saying, *"Woe to you lawyers! For you have taken away the key of knowledge. You did not enter in yourselves, and those who were entering in you hindered."* What was this key of knowledge? Because it was taken away, it hindered the religious from entering into a revelation of the gospel of the Kingdom as well as those who were coming into a revelation of the Kingdom.

The Pharisees were symbolic of three things: religion, tradition, and legalism. These things are exactly what is trying to rob the church today from experiencing the beauty and life of the Kingdom. Religion, legalism, and tradition that are exalted above the knowledge of Jesus Himself and the life that He came to give, are the very things stopping so many from encountering the reality of Jesus and His Kingdom. When the key of knowledge is taken away, those entering the Kingdom are shut out because this is what gives us the ability to understand and receive the message of the Kingdom of God. In Jesus' day, the form that religion, tradition, and legalism had built was worshiped above Jesus, stopping the religious teachers of the law from recognizing Him as the Messiah. As a result, a yoke of bondage was placed on those who were hungering and searching for truth. It happened then and it is still happening today. The church has not modeled the Kingdom the way God intended and desired. So many in society today are disillusioned with the church and God. Society is looking for those professing to know the truth to model it, and unfortunately, all they have seen is rules, legalism, tradition, and religious exercises. And everyone wonders why the youth of our day are going through such great struggles. Let's model the Kingdom of grace and power to the culture. Be the answer!

Next we will explore some of the essentials of the prophetic and its critical role in assisting you in living a supernatural life.

ENDNOTES

1. "Moravian Falls: A brief History of the Moravians," accessed February 29, 2012, http://www.moravianfalls.org/aboutmoravianfalls.shtml.

2. Jack Hayford, ed., *Spirit-Filled Life Bible*, New King James Version (Nashville, TN: Thomas Nelson, Inc., 1999), "Word Wealth" commentary in 2 Corinthians 9.

3. James Strong, *The New Strong's Exhaustive Concordance of the Bible* (Nashville, TN: Thomas Nelson, Inc., 1991), #G973.

CHAPTER 2

PROPHETIC ESSENTIALS

Then I will raise up for Myself a faithful priest who shall do according to what is in My heart and in My mind....
(I Samuel 2:35)

T HE word *prophetic* is very misunderstood. Mention the prophetic and many people's thoughts jump immediately to end-time doom and gloom prophecy, whether secular or biblically sourced. But I want to simplify it for you. *The prophetic is simply representing the heart and mind of the Father to an individual, group of individuals, situation, or circumstance.* As an ambassador of Christ, you are called to be a prophetic representation of the Father on this earth. As His Body we are all called to represent the heart and mind of the Father, thus making us a prophetic people.

Many people have said to me, "Well, I'm just not prophetic." But that is a lie from the devil himself. Of course he wants you to believe you are not a citizen of Heaven or an ambassador of Christ because it is through this revelation that you take your rightful place of authority and live a supernatural life representing the heart and mind of the Father. Just because you are not foreseeing future events and prophesying directive words to people does not exclude you from the prophetic calling over your life. Because we hear His voice (see John 10:27) and have the ability to recognize it, we become a prophetic conduit used of the Lord.

I hope to dispel some misconceptions of the prophetic for you and thus lay a very important foundation for your spiritual understanding of your role and calling on this earth. I believe that God is going to break some false mindsets that you may have acquired over the years because of the religious system that has robbed the church of her potential in Christ.

So let's break down this commonly misunderstood word *prophetic* through various explanations and definitions.

LISTEN, THEN REPEAT

One of the ways to define the prophetic is speaking on behalf of God. Jeremiah 1:7 says, *"But the Lord said to me* [Jeremiah]: *'Do not say, "I am a youth," for you shall go to all to whom I send you, and whatever I command you, you shall speak."'* This is an amazing example of the ambassadorial life of acting and speaking on behalf of the one true King of kings. God said, "Jeremiah, I speak, you listen, and then you repeat what I say." This is a simple picture of the prophetic—to be a representation of the heart and mind of God through what He tells you to say (see 1 Sam. 2:35). To relay a message from God, though, we must first recognize the importance of listening. God can speak and does all the time, but often His people just aren't listening. This is "Relationship With Jesus 101," learning the art of listening so we can speak what we have heard. We all can listen and speak what He is saying. As John 10:27 says, *"My sheep hear My voice...."* Hearing His voice is part of our relationship with Him, who is the Great Shepherd.

UNDER THE ATMOSPHERE AND INFLUENCE

Numbers 11:25 says that God took the Spirit that was on Moses and placed it on the 70 elders, and they all prophesied. These guys did not normally prophesy; they didn't know how to prophesy; they had no training in "Prophecy 101" with a study manual. They had nothing but the divine influence that was upon Moses. They weren't part of a group of prophets like Samuel led (see 1 Sam. 19:20); but God said to Moses, "I'm going to take the Spirit on you and place it on these elders, and they're going to do what you do. They're going to prophesy." These 70 elders were overwhelmed with the heavy, intoxicating influence of the Spirit, experiencing the supernatural.

In First Samuel 10 as well as in chapter 19, Saul, who was not a prophet, came near the prophets who were prophesying and by just being in the atmosphere, came under the influence of the Spirit that was on the prophets. As a result, even Saul began to prophesy. People took notice and declared, *"Is Saul also among the prophets?"* (see 1 Sam. 10:12; 19:24).

This was the fulfillment of a prophetic directive that came from Samuel to Saul: "When you meet the group of prophets coming down from the high place, playing their instruments and prophesying, you will be changed into a different person" (see 1 Sam. 10:5-6). A few moments in the glory of God can have a huge impact on an individual. Saul, who was not a prophet and who had no idea how to prophesy, when he was around these prophets, a spiritual residue jumped onto him and he began to do what they did.

I'm sure when this was happening to Saul he wasn't consciously choosing to prophesy, nor did he have time to process if this was God or go through his checklist of prophetic guidelines. He simply became possessed and overcome with Holy Spirit. Many commentators and theologians would say that, for many of the Old Testament prophets, this type of experience was a Spirit-induced ecstasy. The prophets became so possessed by His will and power that there was no room for error—there was no place for the thoughts of man to interfere. This type of prophetic experience still happens today and is quite amazing when we get to participate in it.

So to prophesy is to speak under the ruling influence of the power of Holy Spirit. In the New Testament, there is a reason why Paul connects the influence of the Spirit to being drunk with wine (see Eph. 5:18). Drunkenness on the wine of the world causes you to do things that are destructive and temporal and contrary to your nature. Being drunk, filled with, or under the influence of Holy Spirit causes you to live the righteous and supernatural life you are called to live and demonstrate to the world.

When you are filled with the Spirit, you become bold and you will be and do what you may not normally be or do. No longer is your personality and fears an excuse. Just as when you are drunk with wine and you do things that you wouldn't normally do according to your sober personality, under His influence, you do things that are not normal for you. No more is your personality an excuse for what you do or don't do in the Kingdom life you're called to live.

There have been times in my life with the Lord, privately or in meetings, when the atmosphere of His glory and power in the room has been so intense that I have been truly overcome. These moments are not just, "I feel the presence" moments; they are all-of-a-sudden moments when there is a great awareness of Him that is impossible to ignore. Because of this overwhelming sense of His presence, people have had to drag me across auditoriums and carry me out of meetings. I have felt the overcoming presence of Holy Spirit like this for days—it feels like I can't escape the influence of the Spirit. These are very special times with the Lord.

You may be thinking of the scripture, "'But the spirit of the prophet is subject to the prophet' (see I Cor. 14:32), and what you have described seems to exclude manifesting the fruit of self-control." This is the very reason why so many don't like this kind of spiritual language to prove their argument when talking about being overcome with His power and influence. This passage of Scripture is not speaking of the overcoming presence of His glory that may occur over an individual; rather, it is in context of prophesying in order, one by one, when it comes to meeting together for a time of worship and encouragement. Throughout Old and New Testament Scriptures, people were noted to have been overcome with what many theologians call ecstasies of the Lord: from the priests in the temple who could not stand, to Saul prophesying in First Samuel 10 and 19, to Ezekiel in various prophetic experiences, to Saul-turned-Paul on the road to Damascus in Acts 9, to John falling as though dead in the Book of Revelation. Being overcome with His presence is not just a matter of choice and faith, of leaning into what the Lord is doing in a specific time or moment, although that does play a part much of the time. In this context of not looking for these moments in our spiritual life, these types of encounters can be explained as His sovereignty, as being at the right place at a God-appointed time. God is sovereign, and just as He may choose to pour out His glory in a special way in one location and not another, this may also be the case in our own lives. There may be seasons when He does something very specific. We didn't ask for it and we weren't looking for it—but God sanctioned and appointed it.

For example, years ago for 46 hours, I was under the influence of God in this kind of way and it seemed impossible to emerge from (not that I wanted to, obviously). Maybe if I had chosen to and said, "God, I don't want this," then who knows what would have happened. But when God is so evident and real to your senses, who would want it to stop, honestly? It was 46 hours of being overwhelmed by His Spirit. I was totally messed up in the most amazing way. It was one of those milestone moments with the Lord that I'll never forget. .

During these moments of being overcome, it's easy for me to speak on His behalf because it seems like there is unhindered synergy between His voice and mine. The awareness of His love in these moments is so strong, and because of that it's easy to release it to those around you in whatever form God wants it expressed. Living a supernatural life is not only for you; it's for sharing with everyone around you.

THE TESTIMONY OF JESUS

The testimony of Jesus is the spirit of prophecy. In Revelation 19:10, speaking of John and an angelic messenger, the scripture says:

> *And I fell at his feet to worship him. But he said to me, "See that you do not do that! I am your fellow servant, and of your brethren who have the testimony of Jesus. Worship God! For **the testimony of Jesus is the spirit of prophecy**"* (Revelation 19:10).

The foundation of every prophetic word is the testimony of Jesus Christ. If you are prophesying to somebody what you believe is in the heart and mind of God, it should always point the person back to Jesus. In this case, as with John and the angel, we do not worship the messenger but the Source of the message, Jesus Christ Himself. He is the One directing, and no individual or angel should ever be worshiped. We worship the Lord God who is one with Jesus and Holy Spirit.

There is great power in our testimony as well; our testimony is what Christ has done for and in us. To be able to say "I was once that and now I'm this" holds much power and authority. It's easy to argue and debate theology, philosophies, and different opinions on certain topics, but it's very hard to argue with someone's personal testimony. Every time we testify to what Jesus Christ has done in and through our lives, we're actually prophesying the very same thing to those listening. We are basically declaring, "Look, if this can happen to me, it can happen to you." Your victory or breakthrough can be someone else's victory or breakthrough. A testimony paves pathways for legacies, and a legacy is for every succeeding generation.

What are we leaving for future generations? My breakthroughs are your breakthroughs and your breakthroughs are mine. It is good to encourage people to share their testimony of the goodness of God. Many people think a testimony is just someone's history, but history is just history—a testimony is more than that. It's current. Your testimony shares who God is now to you, despite your history. This was my history but this is me now—who has God been for you recently? In the Gospel of Mark, the writer recounts the story of Jesus crossing over the water in the boat with His disciples. In Mark 4:35, Jesus promises His disciples that they will make it to the other side by saying, *"Let us cross over to the other side."* Jesus meant it; they were destined to make it to the other side. He will not call us to do anything that we cannot do or that He will not do through us. The beauty of His nature is that if He speaks it, it will happen; and the provision we need to fulfill whatever it is will be available for us.

Let's focus on the verse that follows, which is not normally highlighted when speaking of this specific passage of Scripture. It says in Mark 4:36, *"Now when they had left the multitude, they took Him along in the boat as He was. And other little boats were also with Him."* The last part of this verse says there were other little boats with them. Were they also caught in the storm? If so, what happened to them? I believe that they were fine and that Jesus knew others needed to see what was about to happen. I believe Jesus' hope was for His disciples in the boat to take authority over the storm, and that's why Jesus was in perfect peace asleep in the boat. He wanted them to realize that if He, their Lord and teacher, said, *"Let us cross over,"* and could be at peace in the storm, then so should they (and we) be able to be in perfect peace in every storm of life. Unfortunately, as was common for the disciples—and sometimes us—they did not see what Jesus was trying to do. Whether we make the right decision or the wrong decision, the consequences of those decisions become a testimony to those around us, whether good or bad.

There were *"other little boats"* filled with people watching what the disciples and/or Jesus would do, and how they all would handle the situation. This experience became a testimony of assurance for many— Jesus is ultimately in control. The more they saw Jesus in action, the more it prepared the way for the New Covenant, the day Jesus would be not only with us and watching over us, but also in us. And if the same Jesus who rebuked the storm on the water that day is now in us, guess what that means for us? We are never without insurance. Our policy has given us constant access to the provision we need for whatever situation or circumstance we face.

Throughout your life there will be many people—little boats—around watching to see what move you will make and how you will react or respond. Our everyday actions guided by Holy Spirit are constantly producing testimony of the goodness of God in our lives. Be a legacy leaver for future generations by modeling a life of the supernatural co-laboring with Jesus in everything you do. The prophetic person not only represents God with the words he or she says, but also with his or her actions. It is important to believe the revelation that you are a citizen of Heaven, enjoying the righteousness of God in Christ. Everything that takes place in the life of the believer in Christ is an opportunity for a great testimony of the goodness of God to be revealed to all those around. See and respond with His perspective and watch what happens all around your life situation and circumstance.

> *Be a legacy leaver for future generations—model a life of the supernatural co-laboring with Jesus in everything you do.*

CREATING BY THE SPOKEN WORD

In the same way that Jesus spoke to the storm and said, *"Peace, be still,"* when you receive a word from the Lord and speak it, it holds the power not only to change the circumstance, but also to create and call things that are not into being (see Rom. 4:17). Genesis 1:3 says, *"Then God said, 'Let there be light'; and there was light."* God brought what was not into being by the spoken word. In Genesis 1:2 it says, *"The earth was without form, and void; and darkness was on the face of the deep. And the Spirit of God was hovering over the face of the waters."* As believers in Christ's finished work for us we have access to the power and ability to create realities by the spoken word. A great example of this happening through the believer is when the gift of the word of knowledge is in operation. The word of knowledge gift spoken about in First Corinthians 12:8 is simply divinely inspired knowledge about a situation or person's life—information that we have no natural way of knowing except by supernatural means. For instance, suppose God says to you that there's someone with a certain medical condition or a specific issue going on, and this is the person's name and what he or she looks like, etc. As Holy Spirit releases you to speak this word of knowledge, that word releases creative power, sometimes instantly and sometimes to initiate a process. God's words do not return to Him void; they accomplish what they are sent to accomplish and prosper for the thing in which they were sent to prosper (see Isa. 55:11).

When you release the word, it agrees with what's happening in the Kingdom realm, then the result and answer are released on the earth in the natural realm. Many stories pop into my mind related to this specific gift and its intended purpose. We have seen and heard spines crack as they straighten, tumors disappear or begin to shrink, totally deaf ears pop open, recreated parts of the body appear, blind eyes open, and so much more—all by the word of knowledge. Jesus is the Source who unveils it, and something always takes place, even if it's not always instant.

The very nature and purpose of the prophetic word is to encourage and build up, according to First Corinthians 14:3. It speaks into the darkness and void of people's lives or into situations. There have been many times in our ministry when people have given their lives to Jesus and were healed because of a word of knowledge or a word of prophecy. Through these channels, Jesus Christ unveils Himself and the love that He has for the individual. When His light and love penetrate darkness and emptiness, everything changes. Once again, the prophetic in its purest form speaks the heart and mind of God into situations and over people. It flows from the foundation of John 10:27, which says, *"My sheep hear My voice, and I know them, and they follow Me."* The prophetic must flow from relationship with Jesus Christ, speaking His heart and knowing what He wants to do in every situation and circumstance.

TWO EXPRESSIONS OF THE PROPHETIC

There are two main prophetic expressions when it comes to the heart and mind of God being relayed. First we have the obvious way, which I have already touched on, *hearing and then speaking.* After hearing something from the Father, then we speak with our mouths what He wants us to express.

The second is our *lifestyle and actions* as a representation of the Father's heart and mind. Romans 12:1 says that we are to be living sacrifices, holy and pleasing to God. That is our spiritual act of worship. A lifestyle of worship is a lifestyle that represents the heart and mind of the Father as His ambassador on this earth. We want our lives to be examples of His heart and mind. When you're on the street and, in love, you hand someone a sandwich because he or she has no food, even if you don't say a word, your actions are prophesying to the person the heart and mind of God—and that's demonstration of love.

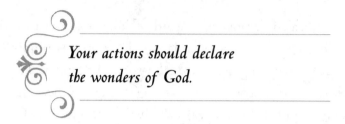

*Your actions should declare
the wonders of God.*

You are prophetic, not just with your voice in what you say, but also in what you do and how you live. Your actions should declare the wonders of God. Never forget that as a born-again believer, you are an ambassador of Christ. The word *ambassador* means to represent another. You are representing the King of kings on the earth. What you do right now is on behalf of another, and His name is Jesus Christ.

> *Now then, we are ambassadors for Christ, as though God were pleading through us: we implore you on Christ's behalf, be reconciled to God* (2 Corinthians 5:20).

Here in Second Corinthians it states that we are ambassadors of Christ—His verbal and prophetic instruments of love and righteousness. An ambassador is a qualified official sent by another country to a foreign land.[1] As citizens of Heaven, we are the qualified representatives of God according to our position in Christ, to represent Him and His Kingdom rule and governance here on earth.

Jesus says in John 18:36 that His Kingdom is not of this world. And as His ambassadors, we represent another world in a foreign land. The foreign land in this context is the earth because our citizenship is in Heaven. The Bible says as born-again believers we are aliens or foreigners to this world (see 1 Pet. 2:11). We, in the current condition on earth, are only here temporarily until we receive our resurrected bodies and return to the new Heaven and new earth (see Rev. 21:1).

As citizens of another dimension, we are to be representatives of the King of the Kingdom in speech and action. This must be the overflow coming from understanding our union with Christ, and not through self-willed effort and religious forms of spiritual discipline. Philippians 3:20 says that *"our citizenship is in heaven."* In the King James Version, the word *citizenship* is translated as "conversation." The Greek word here for "conversation" can be better translated as "conduct." Other translations use "citizenship," which in the Greek is *politeuma*, from which we derive our word *politics.*[2] Therefore, the politics we should be most concerned with relates to the government of the heavenly realm in which we are citizens, and it's nothing like the government of the earth. This heavenly place provides the model for our governance first and foremost, and it is the very source of our spiritual success and eternal life.

I love how my computer's dictionary describes the word *politics* as "the activities associated with the governance of a country or other area."[3] We are called to carry out the activities that directly connect with the affections of the King and His Kingdom rule. We are called to be a prophetic representation of the heart and mind of the Father on this earth. We should desire to represent Heaven by prophesying the heart and mind of God because it's within the potential of every believer to speak to others for their encouragement, strength, and comfort (see I Cor. 14:3). Paul says that we are to *"pursue love, and desire spiritual gifts, but especially that you may prophesy"* (I Cor. 14:1). And in First Corinthians 14:39a Paul says, *"Therefore, brethren, desire earnestly to prophesy."* It is okay to desire earnestly. Don't be afraid to go after what God wants you to go after.

TWO LEVELS OF THE PROPHETIC

We have talked about the two different expressions of the prophetic. Now let's talk about the two levels or dimensions of the prophetic—inspirational and revelational.[4] Let's begin with inspirational.

The voice of God comes through many channels, but it always comes lovingly and to inspire and encourage. And because the New Testament role of the word of prophecy is to encourage, strengthen, and comfort, then every believer is easily able to access this inspirational dimension (see 1 Cor. 14:3). Proverbs 16:24 states, *"Pleasant words are like a honeycomb, sweetness to the soul and health to the bones."* Every believer should be operating on this level in his or her everyday life. Ephesians 4:29 gives the church of Ephesus a charge, saying, *"Do not let any unwholesome talk come out of your mouths, but only what is helpful for building others up according to their needs, that it may benefit those who listen"* (NIV). This is prophetic, and all believers should have this type of communication active in their lives.

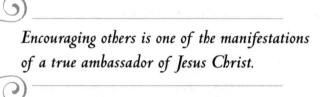

Encouraging others is one of the manifestations of a true ambassador of Jesus Christ.

Encouraging others is one of the manifestations of a true ambassador of Jesus Christ. Obviously some may be more inclined toward this because of how they have grown up or are naturally wired. These people may be what we call the more optimistic types. People who tend to be pessimistic may have to work at being more conscious of their speech, looking to the Lord to give them a right perspective of an individual. According to Romans, there is an actual gift of exhortation or encouragement. Romans 12:8 of the New International Version says, in effect, "If your gift is to encourage others, be encouraging."

So the inspirational level of the prophetic is simply encouraging, strengthening, and comforting and should be functioning in all believers to some degree, even when we may not naturally be an optimistic person, have a gift of encouragement, or walk in a gift of prophecy. Because we hear and recognize the voice of God, we can encourage, strengthen, and comfort those around us. It is part of our spiritual life call.

The second dimension of the prophetic is revelatory in nature. This simply means unveiling or disclosing a matter or specific insight into someone's life, where the spiritual blinds roll up and you see something you never saw before. The person walking in the gift of prophecy falls into this category. It could be likened to putting your shovel in the ground searching for the hidden things that lie way beneath the surface. This level can be directive in nature, bring correction, and/or predict future events. This level of prophecy always must be weighed and judged carefully because if it's not of God, it can be very harmful and destructive. All prophets walk in a gift of prophecy, as it is part of the arsenal they possess that comes with the office (see Eph. 4:11). I believe some people have the gift of prophecy from birth (and I will expand on this later), but the gift is not able to be used in its Kingdom-intended purpose of pointing people to Jesus until the person comes into relationship with Jesus. The born-again experience is the beginning for the gifts of God to be truly used in their redemptive state and purpose. We can also access this gift by faith through pursuit, as Paul encouraged the Corinthian church to eagerly desire the gifts, *"especially that you may prophesy"* (I Cor. 14:1b).

Now if you are a technical-thinking, intellectual, scholarly type, you may be reading this and asking, "How can he be sure that predicting, foreseeing future events, or directive words are the fruit of the gift found in First Corinthians 12:10?" Throughout the New Testament, we see many stories that display this truth. Let me recount just a few from the Book of Acts, where prophecies are directive, futuristic, and predictive. These aren't just little modern-day premonitions; these are insights and revelations from the heart and mind of God to His people.

For example, Agabus, who is traditionally remembered to be one of the 70 disciples mentioned in Luke 10:1-24, prophesied:

> *And in these days prophets came from Jerusalem to Antioch. Then one of them, named Agabus, stood up and showed by the Spirit that there was going to be a great famine throughout all the world, which also happened in the days of Claudius Caesar. Then the disciples, each according to his ability, determined to send relief to the brethren dwelling in Judea* (Acts 11:27-29).

> *And as we stayed many days, a certain prophet named Agabus came down from Judea. When he had come to us, he took Paul's belt, bound his own hands and feet, and said, "Thus says the Holy Spirit, 'So shall the Jews at Jerusalem bind the man who owns this belt, and deliver him into the hands of the Gentiles.'" Now when we heard these things, both we and those from that place pleaded with him not to go up to Jerusalem* (Acts 21:10-12).

Acts 10 tells of an angel who spoke to Cornelius the centurion about Peter coming to them. They were the first Gentiles to hear the gospel message since Holy Spirit was poured out in Acts 2. Cornelius was the captain of the Italian regiment. And Acts 27 recounts the story of Paul's prophecy while on a ship.

Paul never closed the deal and said that only some have the gift of prophecy and others have no access. He left it an open field of potential, saying in First Corinthians 14:1 to eagerly desire the supernatural or spiritual: *"Pursue love, and desire spiritual gifts...."* That word *gifts* is not actually there in the Greek; whenever you see a word in your Bible that is italicized, that means the translators added it at their discretion. So the original Greek says it this way: "Eagerly desire an endowment of supernatural energy."[5] And in that, pursue prophecy because it is considered second to love, the greatest of the gifts. In fact, all the spiritual gifts—gifts of service or office callings—are, and need to always be, a by-product of love. They should all be an expression of love to Him and to those around us.

> *Pursue love, and desire spiritual gifts, but especially that you may prophesy* (I Corinthians 14:1).

Paul did not disqualify anyone when it came to the gifts; he said to desire them. I believe that there are gifts we can access by our pursuit and that there are gifts God has already deposited in us, which we learn to cultivate over time.

Ultimately, your model to follow for this supernatural life is Jesus. If He did it, you can too. John 14:12 gives you a road map. If you just believe, you can do what Jesus did and do even greater works than He did. Always fall back to that truth if you're not sure who you are and what you're called to do. What Jesus did while He was on the earth should inspire you to do the same.

OUR CHOICE

As believers, we have the choice to walk in accountability, integrity, and character and to utilize these gifts for the greater good of humanity, bringing honor to Jesus Christ. God is responsible for all good. He may have given us gifts for good use, but when we operate out of the gift only, not pointing the person or situation to Jesus Christ, we operate independently of Him and we abuse the gift. This is why many people turn away from prophetic-type cultures and environments. What if the person makes a mistake while prophesying? Some think, *What if that prophet is abusing the gift and what if I get all messed up by it?* For that reason, many reject anything remotely prophetic.

You should not operate in fear; fear should never be your decision maker concerning anything in your spiritual life (see 2 Tim. 1:7). You must learn to be wise and discerning, allowing His peace to rule your heart. Romans 11:29 says that the gifts and calling of God are irrevocable—and that's why there can be abuse. For example, there are apostolic leaders who are called to build, advance, and be cultural movers for the Kingdom. But maybe along the way they fall into the deception of sin and fall off the track of their promised destiny. They no longer want anything to do with God or ministry, yet they're still successful at everything they do in the world because the gifts are still there. They may reach a measure of success, but they will not reach their potential. They are no longer stewarding the gifts given for Kingdom purposes. They are abusing their God-given gifts.

Even the wicked are successful. Why? Could it be that God has blessed them? One could argue that the devil has blessed them, but I don't believe the devil is capable of blessing. The devil knows what he can do with the blessing over someone's life—he makes the blessing become an idol that destroys them and their families. What God meant

82

for good, the devil tries to use against them and bring destruction and heartache. The reality is, wicked and bad people with horrible motives still seem to reach a measure of success and thrive. They may not end well or may even self-destruct, but for seasons of time, they seem to live in a measure of what some could deem as blessing. Call that the grace of God or the work of the devil if you want, but it's a reality. I believe that even in the wicked person, God's grace is ever present, in that He is a God of unconditional love for the righteous and unrighteous.

> *...For He is kind to the unthankful and evil. Therefore be merciful, just as your Father also is merciful* (Luke 6:35-36).

> *That you may be sons of your Father in heaven; for He makes His sun rise on the evil and on the good, and sends rain on the just and on the unjust* (Matthew 5:45).

The reality of God's mercy and blessing on the unrighteous then could be the very thing that reveals the goodness of God to them and brings them to repentance and into the born-again experience (see Rom. 2:4).

Think back before you knew Jesus. I'm sure you can identify moments and times when you could acknowledge that your success was not just the work of your own hands but of another force. Or maybe there have been times when you were protected from something that should have killed you—outside of some divine intervention. God is after your heart and life, and He chases those who do not even yet know Him in relationship. David dealt with jealousy toward the ungodly and what seemed to be their prosperous lives (see Ps. 37:1). Sometimes, when things are hard in life, it's easy to forget God's promise to us and start comparing ourselves to everyone else around us.

> *Every good gift and every perfect gift is from above, and comes down from the Father of lights, with whom there is no variation or shadow of turning* (James 1:17).

God gives good gifts, while the devil gives death, poverty, sickness, disease, fear, depression, and the like. Jesus came to give us abundant life, life that runs over with blessing. The devil came to steal, kill, and destroy (see John 10:10). His whole goal is to keep humankind from using their gifts for God's glory. The devil is not able to give anything good, but he does try to keep people from doing good with their gifts.

> *The devil is not able to give anything good, but he does try to keep people from doing good with their gifts.*

I believe that God has sovereignly deposited His gifts in many non-believers and that those gifts will bridge the gap for them to have an encounter with Jesus one day. God's ways are far beyond our ways and His thoughts are far beyond our thoughts (see Isa. 55:8-9). After a person receives the life that Jesus promises, everything makes sense. His or her gift turns into its redemptive state for the purpose of advancing the Kingdom.

POSSESSING THE GIFT

In many ways, the supernatural gifts of the Spirit are like wells that do not run dry. We can draw from them when God tells us to, but it's also part of our responsibility to utilize and steward them. Yes, sometimes in God's sovereignty He initiates a stirring of the gift in His kids for the moment of need, but I also believe that we can access them at will by His grace because we can possess them (see 1 Cor. 14:31; 1 Tim. 4:14; Rom. 1:11; 11:29). How can we develop something that we don't always have (see 1 Cor. 13:2)? If we had to wait on the sovereignty of God every time, we would never be able to become strong in a specific gift of the Spirit. How would we ever become seasoned and mature in a gift if the only way we operated in it was when God dropped it on us sovereignly? If it is only given sovereignly, then how could we be responsible for abusing it or making mistakes? Paul wrote to his spiritual son Timothy to stir up the gifts that were on the inside, those that he possessed and were given through the laying on of his hands (see 2 Tim. 1:6). Because of the access and choice we have to use a gift, there can be more abuse.

In First Corinthians, Paul encourages the church at Corinth concerning spiritual gifts, saying that his heart for them is that they would possess the gifts.

> *I thank my God always concerning you for the grace of God which was given to you by Christ Jesus, that you were enriched in every thing by Him in all utterance and all knowledge, even as the testimony of Christ was confirmed in you, so that you come short in no **gift**, eagerly waiting for the revelation of our Lord Jesus Christ* (1 Corinthians 1:4-7).

There needs to be a place where we can develop and grow and train ourselves in the Lord in these areas. In many ways, the gifts give us access to the revelatory realm, and through relationship with the Lord we can use the gifts to bring honor to the Lord by pointing people to Jesus Christ. It is the Lord's heart that all the gifts He has given us, both spiritual and natural, are filtered through our right relationship with Him. When it comes to the supernatural gifts, if we simply operate out of the gift, not filtering it through the love of the Father and bringing honor to Jesus, then we are not operating any different from nonbelievers who may have similar gifts. God-given gifts are designed to point to a specific destination, and that destination is Jesus Christ. That is the fundamental foundation of the prophetic ministry. The testimony of Jesus Christ is the spirit of prophecy.

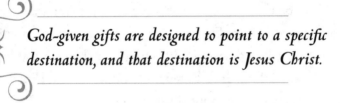

God-given gifts are designed to point to a specific destination, and that destination is Jesus Christ.

Don't worry if you are not currently operating in healing, miracles, casting out demons, raising the dead, loving the poor, or helping someone in need every day—take one step at a time. Understand His love for you and pursue Him, and His purposes will follow. You may not predominantly walk in one area as strongly as others and that's okay. I believe that it's in the heart of Jesus for you to pursue and access all that's available. You may never be a prophet, but you can prophesy. You may not be an apostle, but you can still lead and establish His Kingdom here on earth. You may never have an international healing ministry, but you can see your co-workers and those around you healed.

You may not part the local river near your house and lead millions to safety, but you can still speak to the opposing elements around you and watch them change.

I believe that everyone can prophesy as God speaks, but that doesn't mean that everyone possesses the gift of prophecy. Being prophetic in its simplest form requires relationship with God and the ability to recognize His voice—and we can all do that as believers in Christ. Even nonbelievers who are not into weird ultra-spiritual demonic practices can have accurate prophecies and insights about situations and people. They may not call it a prophecy or even know what they are doing. They don't know how they know things; they just do. In this case, maybe God has bestowed the gift itself to them from the beginning and it's just operating in its unredeemed state at the moment. Remember this important truth: the accuracy of a word has nothing to do with someone being sent from God or not. That is the way it was in the Old Testament, but that is not the benchmark in the New. If that were still the truth, the church would be pretty messed up right now.

Lots of prophecies and future predictions have come to pass from all kinds of different religions and spiritual mediums. If that was our testing grid, we would not be in a good place. Unfortunately, many people in the Body of Christ still live out of an Old Testament testing model, and then get sucked into cults and other faith-destructive spiritual pathways, as we will discuss later. They believe if someone is accurate in their word, they must be from God. That may have been the testing ground in the times before the New Covenant, but when Jesus died and was resurrected, some very important things changed.

I have had the opportunity to minister to many different psychics and mediums. Many of them access the revelatory realm through divination and the demonic realm. Some know they are getting their information from spirits, but some do not. Then there are many who say they have psychic abilities without accessing any hybrid of spiritual beliefs; they just rely on their intuitive sense, which points to the gift on the inside. They know they have some sort of gift because of what they have seen and experienced as they have learned to pull from its resources.

Some of these people are genuinely trying to do good with their gift. But the devil can easily step in and use them as he likes to mock and twist and try to destroy God's creation, especially mankind. There are gifts that I believe God has given me that, if I choose to, I can abuse. Does that all of a sudden discredit the gifts being from God? No. I as a human with a free will can choose to abuse what God has given me. But that doesn't mean my gift isn't from God. Hear what I am saying: I believe that gifts like this are given to us because God wants us to do good with them; but without being redeemed by the blood of Jesus Christ, people end up using their gifts in ways other than their intended Kingdom purposes.

So could it be that many of us predestined in Christ were born into this world with the deposit of some Kingdom gifts even in our "BC" (before Christ) days (see Jer. 1:5)? Could the gifts we possess end up being the very channel through which we experience the goodness of God? It's the goodness of God that leads us to repentance (see Rom. 2:4), so the good gifts that He has given us can become pathways for us to experience His love and forgiveness for the first time.

There is no biblical evidence to state that 100 percent of the gifts of the Spirit, or even of the practical gifts, are given only to the born-again believer. The nonbeliever may have God-given gifts in their unredeemed state at the moment, but it's only a matter of time until that all changes. To say that God only distributes His gifts post-salvation is to say that nothing good as far as talents, abilities, or special gifts can be in the unbeliever. Don't forget that although we are all born into this world in sin—a spiritual prison—it was still God who created us, not the devil and not Adam and Eve. Yes, naturally speaking, when we are born into this world we are born of Adam's seed, which is why we were born into sin, but don't forget who created Adam. Remember too that we were chosen before the foundation of the world (see Eph. 1:4). We all, both believer and unbeliever, were part of God's plan from the beginning. We just need to choose to receive that reality into our lives—that He has loved us and chose us to be in relationship with Him, conformed into His image.

ALL TREASURE HIDDEN IN CHRIST

Unfortunately, the church has not always demonstrated the reality of the supernatural world in its full potential, so perhaps that's why you or someone close to you looked elsewhere to find spiritual answers. Or maybe that's why you never even thought to look at Jesus Christ as your Source for all spiritual knowledge and wisdom. Colossians 2:3 says that in Christ *"are hidden all the treasures of wisdom and knowledge."* But things are changing, and there is a troop rising up who will model the supernatural Kingdom—they are ambassadors of His Kingdom. No kingdom, whether spiritual or natural, is as rich and wealthy as the Kingdom of Jesus Christ. You want supernatural experiences? You want freedom, life, joy, peace, and eternal security? Choose Jesus and His Kingdom. When you receive Him, you become a co-heir with Christ and are given access to the greatest supernatural Kingdom that will ever be. Jesus has so much more for you to grab hold of in your lifetime. Don't sell yourself short just because you want a quick spiritual fix. The devil majors in quick temporary fixes and alternative spiritual ecstasies. Jesus is our eternal bliss and ecstasy and we get to walk with Him in real experiential relationship.

> *Jesus has so much more for you to grab hold of in your lifetime.*

It is God's will that none should perish, and He has sent angels to minister to those who are heirs of salvation—those who are and those who will be (see 2 Pet. 3:9; Heb. 1:14). God is not absent from the dying, broken, and lost; His good gifts to men and women, both believer and nonbeliever, are given to reveal His love, nature, and goodness. As I have said over and over, I believe there are people to whom God has given gifts even before they are believers in Jesus Christ—but it's only a matter of time until they have an encounter with the Giver of those gifts and that gift is redeemed and used for His glory and honor. Maybe I'm talking about you...or someone close to you! It is important for you to have an understanding of the basis for what the prophetic is as we move forward. These prophetic essentials will help build a foundation for the understanding that you are called to walk the supernatural life.

ENDNOTES

1. *New Oxford American Dictionary*, 3rd ed. (USA: Oxford University Press, 2010), s.v., "ambassador."

2. Strong, *The New Strong's Exhaustive Concordance of the Bible*, #G4175.

3. *Oxford Dictionaries*, s.v., "politics," accessed February
    29, 2012, http://oxforddictionaries.com/definition/
    politics?region=us.

4. Graham Cooke, *Developing Your Prophetic Gifting* (Ada, MI:
    Chosen, a Division of Baker Publishing Group, 2003).

5. Marvin R. Vincent, *Vincent's Word Studies*, I Cor. 12:I
    (1886, text courtesy of Internet Sacred Texts Archive).
    Online Parallel Bible, accessed March 1, 2012, http://
    vws.biblecommenter.com/I_corinthians/12.htm.
    Although this note refers to First Corinthians 12:1,
    the same phrase appears in and is applicable to First
    Corinthians 14:1.

CHAPTER 3

THE RELATIONSHIP
FOUNDATION

We love Him because He first loved us. (1 John 4:19)

THE foundation of everything you do in Christ within the gifts or with walking in the supernatural should always be to point people to Christ, and the only way you can do that is by having relationship with God the Father. If relationship with God is not your priority, then you may have divine, accurate revelation or accurate information, but the interpretation, application, and delivery may be warped and thwarted. So often we see gifted people become selfish and seek to build their own kingdom as they operate more out of the gift than out of a relationship with God.

HIS LOVE, YOUR LOVE

The most important aspect of our relationship with God begins with a revelation of His love for us demonstrated in the death and resurrection of Jesus. With this understanding not only will our love spill back to Him, establishing real relationship, but we also are able to love the people around us or, as the Bible puts it, our neighbors. So how do you love your neighbor? Love yourself. How do you love yourself? Know His love for you. He first loved us (see 1 John 4:19), and as we understand this truth, His love spills out so we can love the people around us as ourselves with His love. The Bible says to love your neighbor as yourself (see Luke 10:27). If you don't love yourself, you cannot love your neighbor, and the only way you're going to love yourself is if you understand God's love for you.

In encounters with God, part of Him is revealed to us that maybe wasn't known before. The whole journey that we have with God is about Him constantly unveiling new sides of who He is to us every day. The Bible says that His mercies *"are new every morning"* (Lam. 3:23a), so every morning we get up and there's a new part of the mountain of God that we see. Holy Spirit is constantly unpacking for us revelation of the Son, Jesus Christ. If we saw everything in one shot, we wouldn't be able to handle it.

Right now you may only see one side of the mountain—the side that is comfortable for you. So when someone else has an experience from a different side of the mountain, you don't get it. You don't jive with it. You say things like, "Well, that's not my experience"; you may even say, "I don't agree with that" or "I don't believe that." But remember, you haven't seen all sides of the mountain yet, and one day when you're ready and open to Holy Spirit, you may be very surprised at what is revealed to you.

In Philippians 3:10, Paul's prayer was *"that I may know Him and the power of His resurrection, and the fellowship of His sufferings, being conformed to His death."* Paul had a heart to know Jesus as well as the power—Holy Spirit. Paul wanted the fellowship of Jesus' sufferings. Paul wanted to really know Jesus—not just know about Him but know Him personally. It is desire that leads to a more mature relationship with God, with Jesus, and with Holy Spirit—the triune God.

Holy Spirit is the power Source; He is the resurrection power in the believer (see Rom. 8:11). When you know Him and His power, you will be able to withstand any suffering, trial, and tribulation. We will have trials in our lives. No one's life is perfect and without challenges, but God's grace is sufficient enough to enable you to overcome when you are enduring trial and tribulation. His grace will empower you and strengthen you.

The foundation of real relationship with our heavenly Father begins with a broken and contrite spirit. In conforming, there is great brokenness and vulnerability that has to take place. This is a very important part of our relationship with God that many overlook. Most people don't like being vulnerable or being real and raw with what's going on in their heart. Don't hear me wrong, I'm not speaking of this constant "woe is me" mentality with an introspective awareness that keeps people stuck for years. What I am speaking about is a vulnerability and brokenness that recognizes that Jesus is sufficient and our own strength is not. With His strength we can conquer all.

David was raw and real with the Lord—truly honest with Him. When reading the Psalms, which David wrote the majority of, it sometimes looks like he was a little messed up, like he was on a roller coaster of emotional instability. But yet the Scriptures say David was a man after God's own heart because of his obedience (see Acts 13:22). Vulnerability and brokenness is so vital when yearning to live a supernatural life. Psalm 51:17 says, *"The sacrifices of God are a broken spirit, a broken and contrite heart—these, O God, You will not despise."*

And Isaiah 57:15 says:

> *For thus says the High and Lofty One who inhabits eternity, whose name is Holy: "I dwell in the high and holy place, with him who has a contrite and humble spirit, to revive the spirit of the humble, and to revive the heart of the contrite ones."*

God says He will sit with us—those who have a contrite and humble spirit. We all need to have our daily intake of humble pie. Being contrite and truly humble begins at the cross of Jesus Christ. When we received His forgiveness by acknowledging the price that He paid for our freedom, we truly demonstrated the greatest act and statement of humility. It was reflected in a true understanding of the finished work of Jesus. Honor and recognition of what Jesus has done will always be a by-product of humility, of ceasing from our good works and acknowledging His. It took humility to even acknowledge that we were in darkness and in need of what Jesus died to give us—*new life!* He desires hearts that are open and vulnerable to Him. This does not mean that we are to walk around broken and looking down in the dumps all the time. Some people spend their whole lives in a debilitating phase of inner healing. They never get out of it. There comes a point when inner healing becomes borderline selfishness; our attention is all on ourselves and no longer on Jesus. If we look for stuff to feel guilty about, we'll find it. If we are always looking for junk, we will find it. When this is a person's lifestyle, it becomes a never-ending cycle of so-called brokenness.

God has not called us to live permanently in a self-defeating mode. Rather, there is a healthy brokenness, a vulnerability to be real and able to talk through things, being honest with God and sharing your struggles with the Lord and those around you. Focus on the beauty of Jesus and take your eyes of all the demons that you think are around every little bush and situation. By looking at Jesus, the issues, struggles, and demons that are trying to rob you of life become non-issues.

Years ago when I was in New England in a meeting, I had an open vision during the worship. I looked up to the ceiling of the church where we were and saw what seemed like a portal open up, and then saw what looked like a fireman's pole shoot down through the hole. All of a sudden, hundreds of angels began to slide down this pole. In their hands they were carrying wreath-like crowns. They began to hover over the people in the congregation and began to place these crowns on the heads of the people. I asked the Lord what this was all about and He began to speak to me about how He was releasing the garden mentality back on the people. This was speaking of a vulnerability that promotes intimate relationship with Him with no false covering of shame or condemnation, just as in the garden of Eden before sin came, when Adam and Eve were naked and nothing was hidden before the eyes of the Lord. No awareness of sin or shame was in the garden. The unfortunate reality today is, because false doctrines of faith and religion, the truth of the gospel message that sets a platform for just this has become watered down and twisted. The true untainted message of the gospel is that in Christ we don't have to be ashamed. There is no condemnation in Christ; we have right standing with Him because of the blood of Jesus. We can be totally real, raw, vulnerable, and naked again with nothing hidden.

The sign of a true vulnerable relationship with the Lord is that we can be totally honest and real before Him and those closest to us. We don't have the appearance that everything is good when it is not, covering the junk that is taking place. The religious in Jesus' day did this very well, although Jesus saw right through it all, calling them whitewashed tombs full of dead man's bones (see Matt. 23:27).

> *The sign of a true vulnerable relationship with the Lord is that we can be totally honest and real before Him and those closest to us.*

FRIENDSHIP WITH HIM

We must understand our friendship with God and know in our hearts that we are His friends. Revelation of the heart, love, and friendship of Christ always leads into an encounter. Because we believe we are His friends, we will act, be, and talk differently. After Jesus had been with His disciples for three years, He told them:

> *No longer do I [Jesus] call you servants, for a servant does not know what his master is doing; but I have called you **friends**, for all things that I heard from My Father I have made known to you* (John 15:15).

In other words, friends share secrets with friends. The word *friend* here in the Greek is the word *philos*, and it means a loved one or a beloved, affectionate friend. The verb is *phileo*, describing a love of emotion and friendship.[1] There are emotions involved in this type of friendship.

Some people say, "I don't want to get into the whole emotional thing." I was that way. When I first got saved, I was annoyed at Pentecostal-type people. They bothered me when they got all emotional. It bothered me until I realized through my own encounter with the love of God that God is an emotional God. God created me and you with an emotional place inside. Don't be afraid of emotions because God gave us emotions so we can use them to express ourselves back to Him through worship.

LIVING SUPERNATURALLY IN THE REST OF GOD

What does the rest of God look like? There are two kinds of rest—spiritual rest and physical rest. They are two different rests, yet they are connected to each other. First there is a spiritual rest in God, in His love for you, understanding His grace and mercy, where there is no striving and you know who you are and act out of that place. Then there is a physical rest when you relax from your work like God did on the seventh day of creation. Not that God was tired or needed physical rest, but He did this to set a standard for you and I to follow. We all need a day to rest physically every week, which reflects the constant, ever-increasing revelation of our spiritual rest in the understanding of the finished work of Jesus Christ.

As a believer, you can live day to day in the rest of God when you know who Jesus is and what He did for you. You've been saved by grace through faith, not by the good things you've done (see Eph. 2:8; 2 Tim. 1:9). Your good works cannot get you to Heaven. You can do all the good things possible in your lifetime, and God still will not love you any more or any less. God's love doesn't change for you if you miss your five-minute daily devotional reading on Monday, or your bathroom devotional on Tuesday! Some people go through life feeling guilty, thinking, *I didn't do my devotional last night, so God can't use me today.* That is not living in the rest of God. Constant pressure and performance-driven spirituality produces burnout and stress. That's not God's heart. One of my mentors said to me one time, "Burnout does not happen because of what you are doing, but because of what you are not doing." I agree. God loves being able to reveal more of Himself as you invest your time, but this may come from being still before Him, through conversations in the car, while on a walk, or in study of the Word of God. It just may not only be the five-minute devotional reading; that's only the topping on the sundae.

God desires for us to live in a place of spiritual rest without striving to produce results to impress Him. In many respects, within the church, we have neglected this very reality. In our North American culture, we always have to be doing something. Religious pressure, striving, and busyness all stop us from entering into rest.

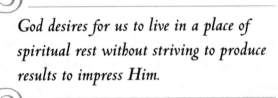

> *God desires for us to live in a place of spiritual rest without striving to produce results to impress Him.*

There was a season in my life, especially in the beginning, when I would go out with the main objective of encountering God. Whether going to the bank, the gas station, or a coffee shop, I would see amazing things, and I always went after them. I was aggressive, and I talked to people about God at electronics stores, grocery stores, etc. There was a season when it felt like everywhere I went, people got saved, encountered the power of Jesus, and were healed.

In the beginning, my heart was totally pure. But then, over time, I got into this groove that if I didn't have an encounter, I felt guilty. I came to a place where if I didn't talk to somebody about Jesus when I could, I felt guilty. When I didn't pray for somebody on the street who was limping or sick, I felt guilty. Then I realized this guilt feeling was a result of not having a revelation of the rest of God. Genuinely it was good that I had those encounters, but sometimes I just didn't want or feel like doing those things. Then the guilt stepped in. I went through a season in my life when God had to work on me and give me a revelation of rest.

Even Jesus took breaks and ate food and did the normal things of life. Even Jesus walked by people who were sick and didn't lay hands on them. Jesus walked by the lame man at the Beautiful Gate every day as He went up to the temple to pray. Only after Jesus died, was resurrected, and Holy Spirit poured out, did Peter and John activate the miracle in that lame man (see Acts 3:1-10). Jesus walked by him every day and didn't heal him. Why didn't Jesus pray for him? I don't know, except that there was an appointed time, and Peter and John fell into it at the right moment.

In the early days of my walk with God, I didn't realize that there is no need to live under the pressure of having to perform to impress God. There was a religious, legalistic sort of mindset that crept in without me even knowing it. I began to strive, thinking that I couldn't just go out to a restaurant and be normal. On the other hand, I knew the opposite could happen as well, where I could become dull and rarely allow God to invade my day-to-day activities. We should be able to push into looking for opportunities, but not feel guilty if we don't.

We need to just chill out with God first, knowing that we are His sons or daughters, knowing that He loves us, and then we can allow our actions to be by-products of the revelation of His rest. When we rest in Him, our motivations become pure again.

We can't keep doing things just because it makes us feel better about ourselves. It's true that when you know God uses you, it makes you feel good. So some people, when they feel like God's not using them, don't feel good about themselves. That is a result of not knowing who our Father is and what He thinks about us. Psalm 46:10a says, *"Be still, and know that I am God."* Just be still and know that He is God. That word for "know" here, in the Hebrew means to perceive and under-stand.[2] God is telling us to be still and know, perceive, understand, and experience Him.

The story about Jesus, Mary, and Martha in Luke 10:38-42 is a good example of this principle. Jesus came to Mary and Martha's house, and almost immediately Mary sat at the feet of Jesus while Mar-tha got busy in the kitchen making food for Jesus. Martha eventually said to Jesus "Don't you care that I'm in here doing this all by myself? Why isn't Mary helping me?" And Jesus, in love, but also with a gra-cious rebuke, said to Martha, "Mary has chosen what is better, and it will not be taken from her."

I hear people say that we need more Marthas in the Body of Christ—that too many people are lazy. That is not true. Nor is it a biblical state-ment. Martha was not doing what Jesus wanted her to do. You can be very busy doing something that you think is for God, yet it may not be what God wants you to do. You could even be busy in vocational minis-try and still not be doing what God wants you to do or focus on for that specific season. Martha thought she was doing a service to Jesus. She was preparing food for Jesus and His followers. Yet, Jesus wanted her to be like Mary, just sitting at His feet in adoration and with a listening ear.

Out of the place of being and resting in God, you will do exactly what God wants you to do. Martha was doing it backwards. She was making food for Jesus, but He wasn't hungry. He wanted her to be with Him. So He said Mary had chosen what is better and only *"one thing is needed"*—to be focused on Him with all of your affections.

Jesus said:

> *Abide in Me, and I in you. As the branch cannot bear fruit of itself, unless it abides in the vine, neither can you, unless you abide in Me. I am the vine, you are the branches. He who abides in Me, and I in him, bears much fruit; for without Me you can do nothing* (John 15:4-5).

A branch does not have to "do anything" to produce fruit. Have you ever seen a branch try to work itself into producing a piece of fruit? A branch grows out of the main vine and it does not have to do anything to make fruit happen or to make leaves grow. The branch just rests in the vine. It understands its role and position in the vine, and it just sits still, so to speak. As a result of just being there, the fruit will emerge at the right time. The branch simply soaked up the sap and nutrients from the vine, and the fruit appeared. The branch doesn't strive or work its way into fruit, saying, "Look at me, vine, I'm working my way into becoming fruit." No, it just is. That's what Mary was doing; she was just sitting there, receiving nourishment from Jesus. Sometimes—many times—that is the most fruitful thing you can do.

LOVE IN THE MIDST OF DARKNESS

In some of the Schools of the Supernatural that we hold as a ministry, we have seen crystal ball healers and people in the occult and other

SECRETS *of the* SUPERNATURAL LIFE

kinds of spirituality have an encounter with the love of Jesus Christ and be totally changed. We hear reports of people of different faiths or spiritual beliefs go through our school by CD and have encounters with Jesus and a revelation that He truly is the true and only way.

Many of those in these alternative faiths and spirituality don't even realize the level of bondage or oppression they are under until they are out of it. Without going into "Demonology 101" or the doctrine of demons, I can tell you that demons do exist and are very real. Not only do the Scriptures reveal much interesting truth about this realm, but I also have personally heard people talk in a completely different voice in languages they don't know while leading them through deliverance. I have seen their eyes change color and their bodies physically contort in impossible positions when demon-possessed—and other interesting supernatural realities. Anyone who has Christ inside and knows his or her authority can cast out demons. The weird belief that you find in those "discover your gift" tests that there is a gift of exorcism is not supported biblically.

There is much controversy surrounding whether or not Christians can have demons, and to set the record straight, I do not believe that there is a demon around every bush. Nor do I believe that demons are the source of every single problem in the world. I think that sometimes believers give way too much credit to the devil and his little kingdom. We need to focus on Jesus, the King of the greatest Kingdom of all, and realize that people are people and will make mistakes. It's not always because a demon made them do it.

Whether you believe that a demon can be in believers of Jesus, on them, around them, or simply just tormenting them, if there is something clearly evil and evident, then deal with it, operating in your authority and privileges as a child of God. If you are a believer in Christ and are one in union with Christ, then demons have no authority over you. If a demon has control of an area in your life, take your Kingdom position of authority and kick the enemy in the backside, sending him back to where he belongs. You need to always remember that you are a new creation in Christ; the old has passed and all things are new. You now possess the key to freedom, so walk in your positional authority in Christ and kick those demons out of your life and out of your way to becoming the person God designed you to be.

You possess the key to freedom, so walk in your positional authority in Christ and kick those demons out of your life.

Just because you're saved doesn't mean you are immune to the lies of the enemy. The enemy is constantly trying to plague the life of believers with lies and rob them of the understanding of who they are as the redeemed sons and daughters of God. So many believers live the born-again life never fully understanding the finished work of the cross and not experiencing the freedom and life that Jesus died to give them. They believe the lie that their spiritual end will be good, but their current life on this earth is still cursed. *Jesus broke the curse* not just for the one day when you get swept up in the cloud, but for every day so you can live in the abundance of freedom found only in Jesus Christ and His finished work.

When Paul said that we are no longer under the curse, he meant it (see Gal. 3:13). The devil can only have authority if given permission, and we give permission when we don't understand our righteousness in

Christ and our role in the Kingdom. Through believing right, our lives will be true reflections of that belief and produce Holy Spirit fruit (see Gal. 5:22-23). Believing that we are still under the curse of the law will produce the fruit of the curse. Believing we have been freed through Christ's payment on the cross will produce fruits of liberation and nourishing Spirit-fruit. Because His love has set us free, we can be that channel for others as well.

Once when ministering on the east coast of Canada in one of my Schools of the Supernatural, during a time of worship before the teaching began, I noticed a young man crying intensely. It appeared to me he was having an encounter with Jesus. I assumed he was a believer in Jesus and knew Him in relationship. As I was transitioning the meeting into the teaching time, the Lord said to me, "I want you to rebuke the spirit of witchcraft." So I rebuked the spirit of witchcraft and carried on, noticing no significant visible changes, but I did feel something shift in the spirit realm in the room.

At the end of the meeting, the young man who had been crying during worship came up to me and said, "Shawn, when you rebuked the spirit of witchcraft, why were you looking at me?" I said I was not looking at him specifically, and we bantered back and forth a bit as he was certain that I was looking at him. If I had been addressing something of that nature to a particular person, I would have recalled where I was aiming the rebuke. But he was convinced and said, "Shawn, when you rebuked witchcraft, I felt a power surge go through my body, and I heard an audible voice speak to me, saying, 'Go bury the tarot cards that are in your bag.'" Then he explained that this was his first encounter with Jesus. God had begun a work in worship earlier, and then he got touched by Jesus for the first time when the ruling spirit or influence over his life was broken. He received Jesus Christ into his life that day and was totally transformed. He buried the tarot cards in a field and was totally changed, and he went with us that weekend on an outreach bringing the love and power of God to the people on the street. The foundation of relationship with God was initiated through the encounter he had.

THE BIBLICAL STANDARD

We need to teach biblically accurate revelation about the operation of the supernatural in our churches in order to see change and balance. Churches will continue to operate in fear and limit their capabilities without teaching and revelation of the heart and mind of God in these areas. Many church leaders do not teach on this topic because they themselves are uncomfortable with it or have simply not experienced it themselves. I would rather be open and bring order when order is needed than to be closed and gripped with fear and lose what the gifts of God were intended to bring to the Body of Christ and to those who have never experienced the love of Jesus. I would rather err on faith than err on fear. You can never fail with faith, but you will always fail with unbelief and fear.

You can never fail with faith, but you will always fail with unbelief and fear.

Years ago I was working out of a mega-church in the United States. I asked one of the leaders, "Why are there no moments where we can just wait on the Lord in a service? There is always something going on." The response, which unfortunately made sense, was this: "We are afraid of someone getting up and giving a false prophetic word." This is exactly why we need teaching. Fear should not be the reason for anything we do or don't do in Kingdom life. But unfortunately this church had some bad experiences in the past, and there was no one to bring teaching and order to some of these areas.

I heard a story of a woman who had come into a service who possibly had a prophetic gift, but was probably wounded by the church or life in general. She was probably not walking with the Lord as she once did. She began to disrupt the service, saying, "God is writing Michelob® on your wall." Michelob® is a beer! She meant to say, "God is writing Ichabod on your wall," meaning "the glory has left" in Hebrew (see I Sam. 4:21). Oh my—she ate some humble pie that day; by His grace, God made it very easy to dismiss her. Maybe she was picking up on something that was happening in the church, but it wasn't her place to do that, and she was not operating out of the heart of the Father, although possibly through the gift. She may have had an accurate revelation, but she totally botched it with the delivery.

This is a good example of why there is fear of the prophetic and the supernatural in the church—and why we need teaching. Beware of people who prophesy to you who are not in any sort of Kingdom community. If I believed the words of every random person who walked in and prophesied something over me in the name of Jesus, I would not be doing what I am right now. That's not to say that God can't use someone like that, but the majority of the time people who walk alone and in no Kingdom community speak out of their biases, hurts, and loneliness, rather than representing the heart and mind of God. They often have no accountability and are not willing to submit to any relationship. More often than not, people who operate independently have a tainted prophetic edge and don't even know it. They call their rejection by the Body of Christ their lot in life. They're suffering persecution for Jesus, when really they may just be socially awkward and people can't seem to get close to them. This is why we need community and each other.

Fellowship helps bring balance to our lives, and it doesn't matter who you are or what gift or calling you may have—we all need real relationships. The Bible encourages fellowship, and the church in the Book of Acts met regularly. Many times these "prophetic" people are bitter at the church and have not generally been accepted, so they see through that lens. The prophetic movement tends to attract really wacky people, but God still loves them. I'm the first to say that God's ways sometimes are just straight up weird. Some of the things the prophets did, as recorded in the Bible, were so incredibly odd, yet supernaturally profound in their fruitfulness and outcome. We may be called to do things that may seem weird, but we are not to be just a weird person who tries to cross the line for the sake of a reaction. Some people are weird for the sake of being weird. God is maturing us in these areas, in order for a pure stream of the supernatural to be released to the Body of Christ.

MODELING THE RELATIONSHIP THAT WE HAVE

Galatians 2:20 says, *"I have been crucified with Christ; it is no longer I who live, but Christ lives in me; and the life which I now live in the flesh I live by faith in the Son of God, who loved me and gave Himself for me."* We are united as one with Christ through what He did on the cross; now He lives through us, revealing His love and nature to those around us. Because of a lack of revelation and knowledge concerning this truth, many in the church do not model this reality. Often what is modeled is a form of religious godliness that denies His power.

Catherine Edwards Sanders writes in her book, *Wicca's Charm:*

> The irony is that often the last people to believe in the supernatural today are the men and women in mainline Christian churches…Wiccans and orthodox Christians may both agree that the supernatural exists, but I learned from my conversations with Wiccans that, in their experience, many churches ignore the reality of an unseen world. Churches become another boring exercise, and in our busy lives, who has time for that?[3]

Wicca is neo-pagan witchcraft and scholars believe it was founded by a British civil servant named Gerald Gardner in the 1940s and 1950s. It involved using ancient gods and goddesses, and ideas about nature worship, and magic. With a few friends and these themes, Gerald and his cronies crafted a new form of paganism and called it Wicca.[4] Many of those in Wicca and other occult practices have, unfortunately, left the church because the true gospel was not modeled to them. They became disillusioned by the powerless church they saw. So they ended up gravitating to something that gave them some sort of visible, powerful experience.

There have been times when God has said to me, "You tell them right now they are going to experience My power, and I will show them that I AM real." This happened once in a bowling alley. A woman started shaking under the power of God right in the bowling alley as I began to minister to her. She was crying and awestruck by what was happening to her. She could not believe that this Jesus whom she had only heard about could be this real to her. This was a milestone moment for her, a fork in the road in her life as she experienced for the first time the tangible love and power of Jesus Christ. Remember, we are the New Covenant tabernacles, so everywhere we go we are called to release the glory that dwells on the inside of us.

Another time I was in Minneapolis ministering on the street, and I approached a very large, tall man. He knew I was a believer in Jesus and tried to intimidate me. As we talked, I learned that he was a Wiccan. As I shared the gospel with him, he began to mock me and said that nothing I told him could be accredited to Jesus and His power. This man said, "I can do those things myself. I can channel energy and heal the sick." He was devaluing the work of Jesus and His reality. Then he said, "Show me and prove to me that Jesus is as real as you say He is." Without any words of knowledge or insight into what I was to do, I began to share testimonies of the power of God that I've seen. He kept mocking me—and he started to agitate me a little.

All of a sudden, a lightbulb turned on in my spirit. So I said, "Okay, let's go, right now, and find someone who is sick. I don't care if the person has no legs or if the person is in a wheelchair. Let's find anybody right now on the street who could be the sickest of the sick. You pray for him first, and I'll pray for him next—and let's see whose God answers."

"Uh, uh, uh, well, I've got to meditate first," he said.

I said, "You have to meditate first? You said you've got it, that you can do all this stuff yourself. Let's go, come on!"

All his walls came crumbling down in one defining moment. He would not go, and he was truly confronted with the faith of a son of God (see Rom. 8:14), someone who didn't only have a mind of faith but also a heart full of faith and confidence in the supremacy of Jesus Christ. I was ready for this challenge and totally believed that Jesus had my back. He is so faithful. I'm not saying you should go out and confront people like this; that was a divine situation, and I believe it was inspired of the Lord. This man quickly backed down, and hopefully he was challenged to reevaluate what he says he really believes. We need to be confident in our relationship with God and model what we have been given.

One time we met a Hare Krishna on the street who was giving people what he called healing massages. As we were talking to him, we found out very quickly that he was open to spirituality but not to Jesus Christ as Lord. We talked to him about how real Jesus is and how He speaks to us. His response was, "I'm not worthy for the gods to speak to me. I haven't done enough yet for them to speak to me." I explained to him, "Listen, there is one true God and His name is Jesus Christ—and He speaks to me all the time. We are only worthy because of His grace and His love. It is undeserved." Then I shared my testimony and the gospel with him. He answered, "That's awesome for you, but it's not for me."

Then the Lord spoke to me and said, "He's got something wrong with his left knee. Tell him I am going to heal him and it's going to prove to him that what you're saying to him is true." After I told him what God had said to me, he said, "Yes, that is true about my knee. How do you know?" I said, "I believe God just spoke to me, and God's going to heal you. I guarantee you 100 percent that Jesus is going to heal you—showing you that Jesus is the real deal." After I prayed for him, he was instantly healed and jumped and ran around in amazement. This man who was giving out spiritual healing massages on the street ended up being healed by the power and love of Jesus. This experience caused him to have a revelation of Jesus and the reality of the truth of the message of the gospel.

The foundation of relationship is absolutely vital if we are going to walk like Jesus did, doing what He did. It all flows from that place.

ENDNOTES

1. Hayford, ed., *Spirit-Filled Life Bible,* "Word Wealth" commentary in John 15.

2. Strong, *The New Strong's Exhaustive Concordance of the Bible,* #H3045.

3. Catherine Edwards Sanders, *Wicca's Charm—Understanding the Spiritual Hunger behind the Rise of Modern Witchcraft and Pagan Spirituality* (New York: Random House, 2005), 23.

4. Ibid., 4.

CHAPTER 4

RECOGNIZING THE
VOICE OF GOD

*My sheep hear My voice, and I know them,
and they follow Me.* (John 10:27)

WE are united with Christ and are one with Him because of His
finished work on the cross, and the premise that the supernatural is for us can be found in this one verse. If we are sons and daughters
of God, then, as His sheep, we *hear* His voice. You may say, "Well, I
don't hear His voice," but that is not true. You *do* hear His voice—you
just don't recognize it. Recognizing His voice is a giant leap forward
into walking in the supernatural.

This is the very reality that Samuel the prophet had to learn as a
young boy.

One night young Samuel was lying in the tabernacle by the ark of God. His mentor and instructor, Eli, was lying down in his place when Samuel heard an audible voice saying, "Samuel!" God called him three separate times, and each time Samuel went to Eli, believing it was the old priest's voice calling to him. It wasn't until the third time that Eli realized it must be the one true God calling Samuel (see I Sam. 3:1-10).

So Eli told Samuel to go back to his place and respond on the fourth time to the voice, saying, "What's up, God? Your servant is listening" (my paraphrase). That was the beginning of the call over Samuel's life to be one of God's representatives to Israel. God had this moment up His sleeve for some time. At the moment of Samuel's call, it had been hundreds of years since a revelation or prophetic experience had been given in that region.

We are all members of God's prophetic priesthood; this is our high calling. For some the platform and influence may be different, and in no way does this mean that all are prophets. Rather, we are ambassadors who do according to what's in the heart and mind of God, according to the call blanketed over the entire Body of Christ.

Samuel wasn't supplied with the latest prophetic teaching CD or latest supernatural book sold in the local bookstore. His experience was new and yet understood by his teacher, Eli. A dark age was over that area, and God didn't seem to be speaking, so this was a new thing to both of them. But all of a sudden God's voice calling Samuel initiated and thrust the young boy into a whole new journey in life.

A lot of Christians are just like Samuel in his pre-prophet days. They are hearing something, but they are not recognizing it as God's voice. Our problem is not in hearing the voice of God, but in recognizing that God is speaking to us every day.

GOD IS SPEAKING

I was ministering on the east coast of Canada one time, and during the meeting I had a vision from the Lord. It was an open eye vision, and as I looked up to the ceiling of the large theater, a giant bald eagle swooped down into the room. I could clearly see its large talons carrying a huge, ancient-looking scroll. The eagle came and stopped right in front of me; he opened his talons and let the scroll unravel. On the scroll I saw what looked like ancient writing in an ancient language. I had never seen anything like it before and did not understand what it said.

I asked the Lord what it was, and He said to me, "This is what's happening in the Body. The prophetic comes but the Body doesn't discern what it is I am saying." We need to learn the language of Heaven so that when the Lord delivers something, we are aware of what He is saying to us. The Scripture illuminated by the instruction of Holy Spirit is one of our greatest tools in understanding the language of Heaven.

We all have our own spiritual grid, and unfortunately it is not always based upon biblical truth but upon fears and past hurts. Samuel heard the audible voice of God, but he still needed someone to help him recognize the voice he was hearing. So how much more do we who don't just hear an audible voice all the time, need teaching and help along this supernatural journey. God may still speak in an audible voice, but often it's just a still, small voice inside, or one of the other ways that He speaks, which we will discover later on. A key goal of this book is to unlock your ability to recognize His voice. This is one of the greatest secrets to living the supernatural life.

*Recognizing God's voice is one
of the greatest secrets to living
the supernatural life.*

ACCEPTING AND ACCESSING

People say things like, "I don't want the gifts. I only want the Giver." Well, that's good if it's genuine in heart, but God wants you to want the gifts too. You can't be afraid of accessing what's in His hand. To the Father, what's in His hand is crucial for you to reflect His face and very nature on the earth. The gifts are like tools in a tool belt to build and advance the Kingdom through the heart and mind of the Father. It would be like saying to a person called to apprentice with an expert for his or her trade, "I only want you; I don't want the skills or tools you offer to be an effective apprentice." We need to learn to receive what is offered by and through the Father's hand.

Some think they are somehow more spiritual and mature by saying things like, "I only seek His face and not His hand." The reality is, in His hand you can see the reflection of His face, and in His face you can see the reflection of His heart and mind so that you can access what's in His hand. We need both, not just one or the other. Since it's been made readily available to us because of the finished work of the cross and the outpouring of the Spirit, we should desire to access what's been made available.

If I made a million dollars available to you, why wouldn't you go after it? If it was there for you to access, why wouldn't you want it?

Would it make you feel more spiritual to say that you earned it all on your own? We need to learn how to access and receive from the finished work of Jesus Christ. His bank access code is simply F-A-I-T-H. Believe that you have it, then take what's rightfully yours because of His grace and mercy. It blesses God when you accept His good gifts.

> *And it shall come to pass in the last days, says God, that I will pour out of My Spirit on all flesh; your sons and your daughters shall prophesy, your young men shall see visions, your old men shall dream dreams. And on My menservants and on My maidservants I will pour out My Spirit in those days; and they shall prophesy* (Acts 2:17-18).

We see in Acts 2:17-18 how God poured out His Spirit, and as a result His sons and daughters and His menservants and maidservants will prophesy. We need this truth to be operating in us at some level as it helps to build up and encourage the body of believers.

Years ago after a meeting, a few of us went to a local coffee shop to hang out together. A woman I had just met at the meeting sat across from me, and all of a sudden I had an open vision. I saw over her head the word *restaurant* flash three times. I knew it was a now-word from God, and I felt she needed to hear it. When I told her what I saw and that the Lord had said to me that it was a good thing, she said, "Oh my gosh," in a really stunned sort of way. She told me that she and her husband had been wondering and praying about buying shares in a restaurant business. This was a sure confirmation for her to take a step forward. At that moment, she was built up in her spirit and was encouraged to move on and take the necessary next steps.

He who speaks in a tongue edifies himself, but he who prophesies edifies the church (1 Corinthians 14:4).

For you can all prophesy one by one, that all may learn and all may be encouraged (1 Corinthians 14:31).

PAY ATTENTION

When it comes to recognizing God's voice, we need to pay attention to repetitions. The first time God speaks something there is an unveiling; the second time is a confirmation and it is established (see Gen. 41:32). The third time, it's time to activate (see Acts 10:16). God called out to Samuel three times. The third time was when Eli knew it was the Lord God trying to get Samuel's attention. This is not to say that you need something to be spoken from God three separate times before you act. But there is something about God repeating Himself when He wants to really get your attention, so pay attention!

In Acts 10, when Peter was in a trance on the rooftop, he had a vision in which God spoke to him to go and preach the gospel to the Gentiles. The vision happened three times, then it stopped. It was like God had to convince Peter. When God showed him the vision the first time, Peter argued with God. This also happened with Balaam in Numbers 22 and with Peter in his denial and his restoration (see Mark 14:72; John 21:15-17), and many other times in Scripture.

Hearing the word of God and then representing the heart and mind of the Father leads people into an encounter with Jesus Christ.

FLEX YOUR SPIRITUAL MUSCLES

If you want to flow and function consistently in the supernatural, you have to stop worrying about your reputation and what others may think or not think about you. Worry and fear will stop you from developing your spiritual muscles. If you want to be the next spiritual Arnold Schwarzenegger, you need to keep working your spiritual faith muscle. It's not really work as in the traditional sense of work; it's simply believing in the person and supremacy of Jesus Christ. Trust me, this is not promoting your works of righteousness—but His, through you.

When I first gave my life to Jesus—in my car on the highway when I was 18 years of age—I had an encounter with Jesus. Then soon after that I lost my job. Next came a season of six months during which I had extensive times of prayer, four to eight hours a day, studying the Word, and learning to recognize His voice.

God then spoke to me about going to the street and sharing with others what I was receiving from Him in my private time. I was a new believer but I learned a lot by taking what God was doing in me privately and demonstrating His love and power out in the coffee shops, restaurants, and streets. I didn't have memorized Scriptures in my brain or tracts in my hands. I didn't even really understand the theology of the cross. But what I did know was that I was a new creation. All things were new and I had a revelation of the reality of Jesus Christ in my life.

I was changed, a transformed man, and it was evident. I would go into the bars and minister the heart and mind of God to people I knew from my past, as well as to those I didn't know. I saw so many amazing things take place. I didn't even really know what the word *prophetic* meant or much of anything about prophecy. Often times something would happen in my prayer time—His presence would overwhelm me in a powerful way. Then He would lead me to go here and go there, and I would always end up ministering to someone and seeing something supernatural happen in an individual or a group of people. God would say something like, "I want you to go to this coffee shop or place at this time and do this or that," and amazing things always took place. This is one of the ways I learned to flow and function in the supernatural. For sure mistakes were made, and there was immaturity on my part. I did a lot of stupid things, but I was just so hungry to learn and grow that I didn't let the fear of failing stop me. So don't be afraid to step out for fear of making a mistake. I learned how to flex my spiritual muscles in this season by just stepping out in faith believing God would use me.

Our responsibility is to lean into the gift of faith God has given us by and through His grace. We need to keep believing in the beauty of the gospel of love and grace continuously, no matter what the circumstance. Although the Bible says we have the mind of Christ, we need to continue to renew our minds daily into that reality for the purpose of a transformed life that is evident for all to see (see Rom. 12:2; I Cor. 2:16).

By the grace of God, we have seen signs and wonders everywhere—in churches, coffee shops, restaurants, hospitals, airplanes, on the streets, and so many other arenas. Anywhere faith is present, signs and wonders will follow. The Bible says signs and wonders follow those who *believe*. Believe in what? Believe in the power of the gospel of Jesus Christ.

Why do we need signs and wonders? Street signs point us toward a destination, and in this case, signs point toward Jesus Christ, our Ultimate Destination. Wonders cause people to be in awe and wonder, drawing them into an encounter with the divine. There are things we won't always understand about signs and wonders, and that's okay. Mystery is one of the most amazing attributes of the works of Jesus in our everyday life. It keeps Him high above, yet plainly in our view.

If everything done under the sun was understood, we could bring Him down to our level. His ways are far above our ways (see Isa. 55:9). The Bible says that God does what He pleases (see Ps. 135:6; 115:3). We don't always have to understand the why, as long as we can recognize Him within whatever He is doing. This does not negate the fact that we need to seek out understanding. Often things hidden are for our finding—and in order to find, we have to look.

A seemingly dangerous prayer is, "Lord, do what You please." The fear of the unknown even plagues the lives of many "seasoned and mature" believers. Sometimes what He pleases is not what we are expecting or what we are comfortable with. For example, read Ezekiel 8:3. It is the story of good old Zeke being picked up by a lock of his hair and levitating between Heaven and earth and then being taken into visions of God. He wasn't just in a vision; he was suspended in midair and taken into visions of God.

Most people automatically assume that the devil has the copyright on levitation and flying, but let me remind you that the devil has no creativity in him. Creativity is an attribute of God the Creator, so the devil just mocks, copies, and distorts all that God has designed and created. I guarantee you that since the beginning, God has been levitating and flying around His heavenly Kingdom. Some Christians are uncomfortable with certain language or buzzwords, such as levitation. Yet when Jesus left His disciples after the resurrection, He defied gravity; and when He returns He will again be defying gravity through levitation and flying (see Acts 1:9-11). Easier-to-accept terms for most people are *ascending* and *descending*.

People need to see and experience the reality of Jesus Christ and His Kingdom. Having good debates and arguments and cool methodology will always have a measure of lasting success, but an encounter and revelation of the love and grace of Jesus Christ will never be forgotten and cannot be argued away. The reality, though, is that there is so much false supernatural activity out there—online and through other media—that we need to bring the true into the midst of all the false. Many times I have modeled this inside and outside the church.

> But *if all prophesy*, and an unbeliever or an uninformed person comes in, he is convinced by all, he is convicted by all. And thus the secrets of his heart are revealed; and so, falling down on his face, he will worship God and report that God is truly among you (I Corinthians 14:24-25).

An encounter and revelation of the love and grace of Jesus Christ will never be forgotten and cannot be argued away.

According to this scripture in First Corinthians 14, God wants any prophetic person who has a word or revelation from Him to prophesy. It doesn't say, "if all prophesy over the unbeliever"; no, it says, *"if all prophesy"*. In other words, as believers in Jesus prophesy over each other, someone who does not believe can walk in and, because of the atmosphere released through the prophetic, end up having an encounter with God.

When you prophesy, you release an atmosphere of the reality of Jesus Christ into the room so somebody who does not believe can come into that atmosphere and all of a sudden fall into an experience with his or her Creator. People will take notice that God is truly present. If all believers were all operating at this capacity, we would see people having more encounters with the reality of Jesus Christ.

I've opened many meetings knowing that the nonbelievers need to see the power of God demonstrated in their midst. One time when I was ministering in England, during the day we went out onto the street to minister to people. We ended up encountering a woman who was a practitioner of Reiki (a form of therapy in which the practitioner is believed to channel energy into the patient through healing hands[1]) and many other various spiritual practices. She believed Jesus was a prophet, a good man, but not the one true way to the Father of all creation. Most people involved in this sort of practice or other various spiritual practices and pathways believe that Jesus was a prophet. They even believe many of the teachings of Jesus, but they do not believe in the supremacy of Christ over all as the writer of Colossians 1:15-20 so eloquently puts it:

> *He is the image of the invisible God, the firstborn over all creation. For by Him all things were created that are in heaven and that are on earth, visible and invisible, whether thrones or dominions or principalities or powers. All things were created through Him and for Him. And He is before all things, and in Him all things consist. And He is the head of the body, the church, who is the beginning, the firstborn from the dead, that in all things He may have the preeminence. For it pleased the Father that in Him all the fullness should dwell, and by Him to reconcile all things to Himself, by Him, whether things on earth or things in heaven, having made peace through the blood of His cross.*

We ministered to the woman and she was definitely touched by the Lord. She saw the evidence of the power of God, but her heart was still closed. She did not yet have a revelation of the reality of Jesus. She seemed very confused about some of her belief systems, which often is the case with many people who believe in something other than Jesus Christ as Lord, the one true medium to the Father. She had beliefs, but they were all over the map.

Jesus was very clear: *"I am the way, the truth, and the life. No one comes to the Father except through Me"* (John 14:6). You can't take a little bit of this and a little bit of that with different faiths, making some hybrid faith, and expect to experience some true kind of spiritual reality. You will experience a spiritual reality, but outside of Jesus by His grace invading, you will experience the lesser, darker reality. Remember, deception can be defined as darkness deceiving by acting like the light. Most aren't drawn to darkness and satan knows that, so he tries to mimic light. Second Corinthians 11:14 says, *"And no wonder! For Satan himself transforms himself into an angel of light."*

It's all Jesus or nothing. There is no other life-giving, eternal Source for true fulfillment.

The woman on the street continued, saying that she didn't believe that Jesus is the only way and that she believed in all these other spiritual pathways. She also said that she had seen supernatural things happen too. Because I was scheduled to lead some healing services at a church, I invited her to attend, as I knew she would see some pretty crazy Jesus miracles right before her eyes. She came to an afternoon session. Unfortunately for her I had planned on teaching about prophetic evangelism and reaching out to the lost. Ha! Of all the meetings to come to, she came to the one on training people how to reach out to people just like her. I said to God, "What do I do?" God said to me,

"Operate out of the Scripture," and He pointed me to First Corinthians 14:24-25, as mentioned earlier.

God told me, "Open the meeting by bringing up five people to prophesy over. She will have an encounter with Me as you prophesy over the other people." It was a powerful time of ministry; the atmosphere in the room changed. God began to move, some healing also began to break out, and by the end of the meeting, the woman was one of the first people to come up to give her life to Jesus Christ. It was amazing.

This is bringing the Scripture to life. It says, *"If all prophesy, and an unbeliever or an uninformed person comes in, he is convinced by all, he is convicted by all"* (I Cor. 14:24). Unbelievers will say, "Wow, God is truly around and among you. I don't want the mixture anymore. I want it all; I want what you've got." That's exactly what happened. The atmosphere of the prophetic and the healing word created brought a greater unveiling to her of the reality of Jesus Christ and His supremacy and Lordship. While talking to her on the street, a seed was planted in her heart. It was watered in the meeting, then harvested.

I encourage you to go to a coffee shop or a restaurant with some friends and prophesy over one another. Then watch the atmosphere begin to change in that place and see what the Lord does. Watch how the atmosphere changes at your table. Watch how people are drawn to your table, asking, "What's going on with you guys? I feel something." This has happened so many times with us.

Moving from a revelation of hearing the voice of God to seeing the importance in recognizing His voice is absolutely vital for supernatural life. Never forget this truth.

ENDNOTE

1. The Free Dictionary by Farlex, s.v. "Reiki," accessed January 13, 2012, http://medical-dictionary. thefreedictionary.com/Reiki.

CHAPTER 5

PARTNER WITH
THE PARAKLETE

*Nevertheless I tell you the truth. It is to your advantage that I go
away; for if I do not go away, the Helper* [Holy Spirit] *will not
come to you; but if I depart, I will send Him to you* (John 16:7).

I was saved about three months and I was going to quite a conservative church. I honestly can't recall Holy Spirit ever being mentioned
as someone on the same level as God the Father and Jesus. I remember
reading the Bible shortly after I had given over my life to Him and His
purpose and seeing the words in John 16:7 that it is to our advantage that
Jesus would go so He could send another. "Another" is the *parakletos*, the
Greek word for helper, guide, comforter, literally meaning one called
alongside to help. He is Holy Spirit. He is the third Person of the triune God, but in no way a lesser part.

I remember getting so excited, thinking, *Wow! This gets better and better. Someone else is coming.* I had no idea at the time that He was already in me. I was still so new and fresh into this whole relationship with Jesus. I began a quest to get to know the person of Holy Spirit. I knew that He was the personality of the Godhead here to guide me and make Jesus known to me in greater ways, to be my tour guide for Kingdom life on earth.

The Bible says in Philippians 3:3 that we worship by the Spirit and in the Spirit, so I wanted to understand this third Person of the triune God. Second Corinthians 13:14 says that the Holy Spirit communes with us. What did communion with Holy Spirit look like? I began to study and seek the Lord. During this process, I was scheduled to play the drums at a men's retreat. I ended up in a room with 12 guys in bunks, and I had a dream. I can't remember the details of the dream other than I know it was about Holy Spirit.

All of a sudden I woke up out of the dream, my body shot up out of bed, and I was repeating these words over and over again, without my control, "Do we really know God's Spirit, do we really know God's Spirit, do we really know God's Spirit." It was such a powerful experience; the power of God was all over me. I was hoping that I didn't wake up anyone, and I went back to sleep. As I sought more understanding that week, I received a book from someone. I remember opening the book one night and the first thing I read was this, and it absolutely blew me away:

> We think we know where God lives. We think we know what He likes, and we are *sure* we know what He dislikes. We have studied God's Word and His old love letters to the churches so much that some of us claim to know *all* about God. *But now people like you and me around*

the world are beginning to hear a voice speak to them with persistent but piercing repetition in the stillness of the night: "I'm not asking you how much you know about Me. I want to ask you, 'Do you really know Me? Do you really want Me?'" [1]

This was pretty much my experience at the retreat that night almost verbatim, and I knew something was going to happen to me. One night the following week, I was in my car, and I received the baptism of Holy Spirit and began to speak in this amazing unknown language called tongues. My spiritual life was lifted to new heights from that day on. Just to clarify, I believe that the purpose of the baptism of the Spirit is to be a witness to the finished work of the cross through Christ (see Acts 1:8), not to speak in tongues. I just happened to have them both come at the same time.

This experience set me on an aggressive pursuit for the power of the Spirit to be active in my life and to establish a life of intimate communication with Him. The Bible says we can't know the mind of the Father—it is the Spirit who searches all these things. No one knows what God is thinking except the Spirit of God: *"For what man knows the things of a man except the spirit of the man which is in him? Even so no one knows the things of God except the Spirit of God"* (1 Cor. 2:11).

As believers in Christ, we have access to every part of our promised inheritance while we live on the earth. The Father has given talents, gifts, and many spiritual blessings. We are destined to be blessed because of what Christ has done. We are co-heirs with Him, and all that He has He has shared with us. Paul talked about one of these personal blessings and gifts in First Corinthians 14—our personal, heavenly prayer language. There is a distinct separation between the public use of what the Bible calls the gift of tongues with interpretation and the personal, private use of the gift of tongues for personal edification of our spirit.

There is much controversy over the manifestation of both the corporate use and private use of this prayer gift. The devil likes to grab hold of important truths for believers and insert wedges of strife and fear to create chaos and disorder. He knows that if people do not utilize this gift, he will have one less thing to worry about. Worry and anxiety define the devil because he knows that, in the end, we win. He does whatever he can to prolong his end, which means hindering believers and nonbelievers alike from truly possessing their God-given inheritance in Christ.

Years ago during a ministry trip in Dayton, Ohio, one of the pastors told me that another pastor challenged him, saying, "Unless you pray in tongues at least one hour a day, you will not access the supernatural on a consistent basis." Biblically this cannot be proven, although Paul does make comments to the church at Corinth about tongues. It does make you think about it practically. If your personal prayer language is used to build up your spirit as Paul mentions in First Corinthians 14:4 and 14, then your spirit is strong and you would probably have greater clarity when recognizing His voice.

I accepted the challenge. At the time, I was traveling as an intern with a couple whose ministry was based in Minneapolis, Minnesota. My mentor said he wanted me to prophesy over the people that night. So I thought, *What a great opportunity to try this tongues thing out.* I prayed in tongues normally, but never until that point for more than about 10 minutes. After the first 15 minutes, I was praying in English again and battling some major distractions. It seemed so unproductive and felt like I wasn't accomplishing anything in prayer.

At this point, I was saved just over a year, and I was so hungry to grow and move forward in my walk with Him. My mind was telling me that what I was doing was irrational and illogical—*Why don't I pray something that makes sense.* I kept bringing my focus back to trying to accomplish a task because, in the beginning, that is what it felt like. At some point, though, something shifted. I cannot tell you what it was, but probably around the one-hour mark, I could feel strength rising in my spirit.

When I got to the meeting, a whole new realm had been opened to me. When I looked at the people in the meeting, God gave me detailed words of knowledge and detailed insight into their lives—because I believe my spirit was so strong and built up. We can't forget this was a gift that Paul encouraged us to walk in and steward, even to the point where it seemed as if he was bragging about how much he spoke in tongues. Paul says in First Corinthians 14:5, *"I wish you all spoke with tongues...."* And in First Corinthians 14:18, Paul says, *"I thank my God I speak with tongues more than you all."*

I am in no way making an absolute statement that if you don't pray in tongues, you won't access the supernatural in your life. Jesus is our doorway first and foremost—not speaking in tongues. But I believe the Word when it says that if we pray in tongues, we build up our spirits, and if our spirits are built up, we will have an easier time building up others.

> *I believe the Word when it says that if we pray in tongues, we build up our spirits, and if our spirits are built up, we will have an easier time building up others.*

Many people think it's sacrilegious to pray in tongues when you are not in a church setting or that it is a sovereignly inspired gift that happens only at certain moments. This is not true. It is used for personal edification and is something you have and can activate at any moment to build up your spirit. Pray in tongues when you're in the shower, in traffic, while making dinner—incorporate this gift into every area of your life, and watch what begins to happen.

SEAL OF THE SPIRIT

*In Him you also trusted, after you heard the word of truth, the gospel of your salvation; in whom also, having believed, **you were sealed with the Holy Spirit** of promise, who is the guarantee of our inheritance until the redemption of the purchased possession, to the praise of His glory* (Ephesians 1:13-14).

Because of the seal of Holy Spirit on our lives as believers, we now have the mind of Christ (see I Cor. 2:16). Our contact to this reality is by Holy Spirit; it is spirit-to-Spirit contact, our human spirit with His (see Rom. 8:16). Through Holy Spirit we unpack the mind of God and begin to see like He sees. He is our Spirit Guide, guiding us into all truth, searching the deep things of the Father, and grabbing hold of the mind and thoughts of God—then unveiling and bringing them to us. He is the One who unveils Jesus Christ to us—to you. Holy Spirit's job is to reveal Jesus, and Jesus reveals the Father (see John 16:12-15).

We need to tune into Holy Spirit who is searching the thoughts and the deep things of God regarding our situations and us, for Holy Spirit is in us and with us:

*But if the Spirit of Him who raised Jesus from the dead dwells in you, He who raised Christ from the dead will also give life to your mortal bodies through **His Spirit who dwells in you** (Romans 8:11).*

We are the temple of the Holy Spirit, Paul says in First Corinthians 6:19. He is not that far-off entity that we can't reach. He wants to move through us, in us. There are times when we know the moment we lay hands on someone that he or she will feel and encounter the power of God—because Holy Spirit lives inside us. Resurrection power is within us.

INTIMACY WITH HOLY SPIRIT

Let's talk about what Holy Spirit is not. He's not a liquid; He's not an it. He's not a lesser Person of the Trinity or a weird spirit; He is not boring, a people pleaser, rude, a respecter of persons, selfish, or unsatisfying. He is not someone who puts up with sin. He's not emotionless, and He's not many other things that people think He is.

Holy Spirit is the One who fellowships and communes with us; He is our Guide, Teacher, Counselor, Friend, Comforter, Helper, Empowerer, Leader, God Himself, and Worship Leader, according to Philippians 3:3. He is the personality of the God who was sent to the earth to be in us and to teach us all things. Second Corinthians 13:14 says, *"The grace of the Lord Jesus Christ, and the love of God, and the communion of the Holy Ghost be with you all."* The grace of the Lord Jesus Christ is His forgiveness and His death that bought our freedom, destroying sin, sickness, and disease. Grace is also the power that enables you to overcome the dominion of sin through what He did on the cross. The love of God is shown in sending His Son into the world to die.

The communion of the Holy Ghost is about the intimate seal that we have with Him, revealing the very nature of Jesus to us day after day. This reality was given after Jesus left the earth. The word for "communion" in Second Corinthians 13:14 is *koinonia* in the Greek. It means partnership and/or social intercourse—an intimate kind of conversation that goes past the surface, connecting you at a deep level.[2] Communion is about fellowship and contribution. You're contributing to your relationship; you're investing in your relationship and, as a result, there's a return. It's a two-way relationship. In the *Funk and Wagnalls Standard College Dictionary*, commune or communion means to confer or converse intimately, to have intimate conversation.[3] The word for "communion" in this Scripture passage means having or sharing something in common, a mutual sharing of thoughts or feelings. Often you are attracted to those who like the same things that you like; you can share the similarities you each have in communion and fellowship. With Holy Spirit, it's much the same. The similarity starts with Christ being the central focus. Holy Spirit is the One who unveils Jesus to us more and more all of the time. Your revelation of Christ now will not be your revelation of Christ two years from now. Holy Spirit is constantly unpacking more of Jesus to us every day throughout our life journey. There should be a deeper unveiling of the heart and beauty of Christ as you mature. The more you commune with Him, the greater Jesus becomes to you. Kathryn Kuhlman said, "The Holy Spirit is more real to me than any human being."[4]

We must understand the importance of getting to know Holy Spirit who unveils Jesus to us continually. He is the One who searches the mind of God, and He is the One who makes the thoughts of God known to us (see 1 Cor. 2). He is the One who searches the deep things of God. We need to know His heart, know Him, the person of Holy Spirit.

The attributes of Holy Spirit, of the Son, and of the Father are different. We see the different functions in Scripture, yet they are all One—just as we are made up of three parts, according to Scripture: body, soul, and spirit. Jesus, speaking to His disciples, says in John 16:

> *I still have many things to say to you, but you cannot bear them now. However, when He, the Spirit of truth, has come, He will guide you into all truth; for He will not speak on His own authority, but whatever He hears He will speak; and He will tell you things to come. He will glorify Me, for He will take of what is Mine and declare it to you. All things that the Father has are Mine. Therefore I said that He will take of Mine and declare it to you* (John 16:12-15).

Holy Spirit's job is to make known to you who Jesus is, to unveil Jesus to you. Often when you have a dream and there's someone you recognize but can't put your finger on who He is, yet you know He's there, or the person appears as a guide; most of the time, that is Holy Spirit. He doesn't come on His own behalf; He comes on behalf of Christ to reveal Christ to you.

UNDER THE POWER

One time during a meeting I was leading, we were seeing incredible miracles take place—deaf ears opening and many being touched by His love and power. It was one of those wild, crazy, powerful milestone meetings. While these things were all taking place, Holy Spirit said there was someone in the room who did not know Jesus in relationship. This was not a jam-packed meeting and most of those attending were believers in Jesus. But Holy Spirit said, "You need to stop what you're doing and make a call for that one individual who does not know Jesus, and tell him that he is going to experience the power of God in his body right now." A young man came forward, and as he did, I said, "Before we do anything, you're about to encounter the power of God right now in your body."

All of a sudden the power of God came on him and he began to shake and cry. The place went nuts because many of them knew who he was. Even before he confessed that Jesus was Lord, he had an encounter that altered the course of his life forever. When you understand the power of Holy Spirit in you, amazing supernatural works will begin to happen. The Spirit who raised God in the flesh from the dead is in you right now. What a powerful Kingdom truth. We didn't just get a portion or percentage of Holy Spirit and His power, but the fullness. To believe that one person has 10 percent of the Holy Spirit and someone else who fasts and prays has 50 percent of the Holy Spirit is such a wacky, heretical belief. The born-again experience sets us all on an equal playing field. Although our responsibilities, callings, and gifting may differ, we do not have a junior Holy Spirit or a senior Holy Spirit because of good works or because of our faithfulness—we have Him, period. The fullness of God dwelt in Jesus Christ bodily, we are in Christ, and Christ is in us; therefore, we possess the fullness of God (see Col. 1:19; 2:9).

We didn't just get a portion or percentage of Holy Spirit and His power, but the fullness.

THE MORE AVAILABLE

We must learn by the renewal of our minds and by revelation of who we are as sons and daughters of God how to access what's available to us. Just because we have the fullness of God doesn't mean we are accessing the potential within us. The same goes for our authority in Christ. According to Scripture, all authority has been given to us, but we grow into what has been given through the process of time. Our inheritance in Christ to us can be compared to a wardrobe or closet full of clothes. As we grow, we grow into what's already there. Holy Spirit is constantly revealing every day understanding of the vastness of the inheritance we have in Christ. He is causing us to continue to grow into all that God has prepared for His children as His heirs of the Kingdom. As a newborn baby, your body wouldn't fit appropriately into a pair of pants made for a ten-year-old. The pants wouldn't fit, and, in fact, could be a hindrance and distraction. God knows what fits us, and that's why this spiritual journey with Christ is progressive. We are constantly unpacking the truths and experiencing the inheritance that has been set out for us to walk in. Faith, stewardship, and maturity all draw on the more that's already been given and made available to us in Christ. We are constantly growing into what's been freely given by and through the cross of Christ. So I have good news for you: you have it all right now!

You cannot get any more of God than you already have as a new creation, a born-again believer. As you grow, you begin to experience more and access more. You have all the provision you'll ever need in your heavenly bank right now; but right now you may only be accessing $10 (see 2 Pet. 1:3). As your revelation of God's love increases, represented in and through Jesus, you begin to realize what you truly have available to you. You see that you have a million dollars in your account, so no longer are you just making $10 withdrawals, but way bigger withdrawals. You now know the resources available to you. Through the knowledge of what you have in Christ, you will begin to access the more that's been given to you in Christ because of His grace.

REVEALING GOD'S THOUGHTS

Knowing Holy Spirit and tuning into Him is the key to knowing God's thoughts and feelings toward others and ourselves. Psalm 139:17-18a says, *"How precious also are Your thoughts to me, O God! How great is the sum of them! If I should count them, they would be more in number than the sand."* To practice speaking the heart and mind of the Father, ask Holy Spirit to grab one of the millions of thoughts He has toward a specific individual. We may only receive some of His thoughts, not all of them, *"For we know in part and we prophesy in part"* (I Cor. 13:9). We won't know everything, but we will receive pieces of information. There have been times when I've asked Holy Spirit to give me insight into someone's life. After I received the pieces He revealed to me and shared them with the individual, then all of a sudden, they all made sense as they came together. Sometimes you just need to open your mouth and all the words that need to come out do so, with perfect synergy.

We need to make sure faith is in operation in everything we do, but especially in this area. Prophecy works through faith, sometimes by believing the little you have from the Lord will grow as you open your mouth. In many ways, it takes time to become seasoned. It's a sense that is developed over time. Confidence and faith in the reality that God will speak flows through practice and learning to work with and trust Holy Spirit. Faith is always the avenue of access to the supernatural and the Kingdom. We know that Christ is the doorway; He is Jacob's ladder; He's the bridge, the mediator to everything good in eternity. And He desires faith, us believing in who He says He is, what He says He will do, and what He promised to do through us. We need to walk forward and step into the supernatural and prophesy according to our faith. By God's grace, He has dealt to each one a measure of faith (see Rom. 12:3).

A MEASURE OF RESPONSIBILITY

With that measure of faith comes responsibility. We have to be responsible with what we have—too many want to bypass the learning part. If we want to mature, we need to keep in step with Holy Spirit. Holy Spirit is in a different step with every individual according to his or her season and where each one is on his or her spiritual journey. It would be unfair to expect a new believer to be at the level of a ten-year-old believer—even though sometimes new believers are more mature than older ones.

If you only have faith right now to say, "Jesus loves you," then work that revelation and practice it wherever you are—at work, the grocery store, mall, coffee shop, restaurant, wherever. It's okay. You need to start somewhere. You don't have to wait for supernatural boldness to come on you; begin to work that muscle of faith now and let His boldness develop in you.

Of course, we need to walk in His supernatural boldness as well, don't get me wrong. Some people just need to hear that Jesus loves them—right now. But because some Christians are locked in their room praying 12 hours a day for boldness, they may be missing divine opportunities. I'm not diminishing prayer; if that's the season God has called you to, then do it. In fact, I'm a major advocate of prayer like that and have done it and still do. Let's just not forget the simple yet profound ways available for reaching out to people.

Be honest with yourself and focus on the areas where your heart is drawing you and you have faith to see a breakthrough. Then let faith grow in and through you to go after the more that you have available. Every time you see a new miracle, you lose your right to not believe for that same miracle to happen again. In other words, faith grows into a massive tree of influence and power—if you allow it. Nurture your faith, watch over it, let Holy Spirit blow over you with His presence and power and word daily, reminding you of your prophetic promise of destiny on this earth because of what Christ has done for you.

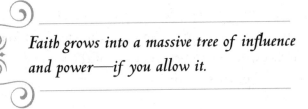

Faith grows into a massive tree of influence and power—if you allow it.

I have grown into a stronger faith now than what I had two, three, four, five, or six years ago, etc. While believing for the little and seeing the Lord fulfill His promise, I now have faith for the *much* that seemed so impossible to believe for years earlier. Part of the reason for this is because of our level of revelation of who Christ is. The way you see Christ and what you experience today will not compare to the future five or ten years down the road.

We are moving from glory to glory, constantly growing and developing. The truth of our positional reality in Christ is supposed to determine our conditional, temporary reality on this earth. This truth is not reality for many because they don't understand or truly believe in what Christ died to give them. He became our substitute and put us up in His heavenly penthouse. He put us up where He is after His resurrection. We sit with the Prince of Peace Himself. We're positioned in prosperity because He is the Prince of Prosperity. He is the Prince of Shalom. (See Ephesians 2:6; Isaiah 9:6.)

The level of revelation you have of Jesus and His finished work for you determines the level of His promised inheritance for you on this earth that you access and experience. That is why we need to be renewed in our minds and constantly keep our heads in the clouds. We want and need to see everything through the eyes of Jesus. I have often heard people describe some Christians as "too heavenly minded and no earthly good." I believe that statement is heresy. It is one of the most unbiblical statements that I hear. The truth is, we are supposed to be so heavenly minded that we are only earthly good. Jesus was the perfect example of this.

Jesus did only what He saw His Father doing; He could do nothing on His own initiative (see John 5:19). He was about His Father's business and only said what He heard His Father say (see John 8:38). His spiritual nourishment of food was not of this earth; it was to do the Father's will on the earth: *"Jesus said to them, 'My food is to do the will of Him who sent Me, and to finish His work'"* (John 4:34). How did He do the will of the Father? By keeping His focus on heavenly realities, where He would one day be seated, at the right hand of His Father.

Paul encourages the believers at the city of Colosse to keep their minds focused on heavenly realities. There is a reason for Paul's encouragement—we reflect what we look at constantly. What we behold changes everything. That is why we need to be constantly reminded of our inheritance in Christ, that we are co-heirs with Him. We do this by focusing our attention and affections on His beauty, goodness, and faithfulness. Our revelation of who Christ is to us determines much of our experience—or lack thereof. If you don't believe that God wants to heal people, then you won't pray for people to be healed, and it could be assumed you don't really believe the gospel message. Some like the salvation part but not the healing part.

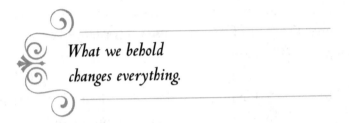

What we behold changes everything.

When you accept the revelation that He wants to heal people, you will begin to step out and pray for people to be healed. As you do, you will see it happen. That's a promise (see John 14:12). You may not have faith right now for God to give you a car, but you may have faith for God to give you $100; and rest assured, that's okay. There is no condemnation; just don't sell yourself short of the heart of God for you. Maybe one day God wants to give you a car, and so through time and as He renews your mind, you'll have the faith to actually believe for God to give you a car. I believe people don't access more and they don't receive more because they don't ask—they're afraid to be in faith for specific things or needs. Many think, *I can be in faith for this, but not for that. I can be in faith to pray for somebody to be healed, but I'm not in faith to believe God wants to provide a way for me to pay my bills.*

We say practical things like, "God gives us a job to provide for our needs." We know that we need to be wise with our resources, and it all sounds good and responsible. There is truth to all of that— God does bless us with jobs. But the main purpose of that job is not money. Surprise! There is a Kingdom purpose that is always first and foremost, and money is only an added bonus. Money is never the main thing connected with our jobs—the Kingdom is. Your career is not a moneymaker. It's supposed to be a Kingdom pusher, with money and provision following that reality and purpose. First Corinthians 4:2 in the Amplified Bible says, *"Moreover, it is [essentially] required of stewards that a man should be found faithful [proving himself worthy of trust]."* We have to become faithful stewards of what God has given us and choose to walk in faith. Even though faith is a gift, we have to choose to unwrap it day after day. This is our measure of responsibility fueled by the reality of partnering with Holy Spirit.

GOOD FOR YOU BUT NOT FOR ME

Years ago we were doing an outreach during the day while a conference was going on. We saw some incredible things—more than a dozen people had an encounter with Jesus and were born again right on the street. This all happened through prophesying the heart and mind of God and interpreting people's dreams on the street. It was so powerful; people were weeping and getting totally touched by Jesus! One man came and sat down with us, and we began to prophesy over him. God started to reveal His heart for the man to us. We could tell that Jesus was working on his heart, but he was still hardened to the reality of Jesus being the real deal.

We could tell he was the kind of guy who thought, *C'mon, show me what you've got.* He was very skeptical. As we ministered to him and demonstrated God's love for him, he said, "Yeah, I don't believe that this is all Jesus," and, "This whole Jesus thing is good for you, but not for me." All of a sudden, a word of faith popped up into my spirit. Holy Spirit said to me, "Tell him that in three days from now he is going to meet somebody who is going to tell him everything that you've just told him, that I AM the only Way, and that will confirm to him that everything you are saying to him is true." So immediately I told him what I felt Holy Spirit spoke to me. In my mind, though, I was thinking, *What did I just say? I live about six hours away from here—what are the chances of me seeing him again?*

Four days later, I was still in that town sitting at a coffee shop, writing—and in walked that same guy. I laughed on the inside and thought, *This is definitely a God moment.* I approached him to say hi, knowing he would remember me. Then I asked him, "So did anything happen yesterday?" He said, "Actually...yeah." He told me that the day before he happened to see a high school friend with whom he used to party. His friend told him about his encounter with Jesus and how his life was changed. Then the friend invited him to church. He then told me that his friend was saying all the same things that I had told him three days earlier. The Lord fulfilled His word, and he left with a revelation of the truth and reality of who Jesus is. In that moment, he knew that what I told him could not be passed off as chance, coincidence, or good karma, but had to be a word from God—the love and promise of Jesus to him.

NOT A VENTRILOQUIST

When it comes to moving in faith and stepping out into these areas of supernatural Kingdom life on the earth, we need to understand a very important principle of truth. Holy Spirit does not move our mouths and flap our jaws and drag us on a leash into obedience to what He is saying to us or telling us to do. I believe there can be times, and this is even seen biblically, when Holy Spirit overwhelms you in such a way that He overtakes your body and senses. Look what happened to Paul in Acts 9:3; he didn't have a choice about getting totally whacked by the Lord—it was a sovereign encounter. And look at King Saul in the Old Testament who prophesied in an ecstatic state of the Spirit all night and day, and then took off his clothes. He wasn't a naked prophet; he just got overwhelmed by the ecstasy of the Lord and probably could not have come out of that place if he wanted to (see I Sam. 19). Holy Spirit had a plan and purpose.

Having encounters with Holy Spirit will, most of the time, be the result of you choosing to lean into what He is doing, and then stepping out in faith. He wants to give you a determined kind of faith. Ezekiel was a great prophet to Israel. God said to Ezekiel, *"You shall speak My words to them* [rebellious Israel], *whether they hear or whether they refuse, for they are rebellious"* (Ezek. 2:7). God had already reminded Ezekiel that the people's hearts were hard, so they wouldn't hear him. Now imagine God spoke to you and said He had hardened the hearts of the people or person He wants you to minister to and he or she won't listen to you. This was the case with Ezekiel as well as with Moses. God had hardened Pharaoh's heart, yet God told Moses to go to Pharaoh and tell him what God was saying.

To our natural selves, it wouldn't really make much sense to do something when even God Himself says He has hardened the hearts of the individuals. But if He says to go there, then there is a reason beyond what we can see with our natural eyes and minds. It's a matter of faith initiating obedience. God thought in His heart, *Even if they refuse, and actually they are going to refuse, Ezekiel, you keep speaking My words to them because My words do not return to Me void. In your eyes right now they may look like the words are not penetrating, but eventually they will. Do not let your obedience to My word be dictated by a person's refusal to listen to the word that I'm giving you to tell him.*

Ezekiel 3:8 says, *"Behold, I have made your face strong against their faces, and your forehead strong against their foreheads."* That literally means God was saying, "Ezekiel, your determination to prophesy must be stronger than Israel's refusal to listen."[5] Determination to step out in faith, access the Kingdom, and release His word to somebody must be stronger than the fear of failure and seeing nothing happen with the words that He has given you. When it's from God, you may not see the fruit now, but you or someone else will see it eventually.

Isaiah 55:11 says:

> So shall My word be that goes forth from My mouth; it shall not return to Me void, but it shall accomplish what I please, and it shall prosper in the thing for which I sent it.

Understanding our role in partnering with Holy Spirit, leaning into His promptings, and unveiling Jesus to people is absolutely what the supernatural life looks like, and He is inviting all into this truth and experiential reality.

ENDNOTES

1. Tommy Tenney, *The God Chasers* (Shippensburg, PA: Destiny Image Publishers, 1999), 1.

2. Strong, *The New Strong's Exhaustive Concordance of the Bible*, #G2842.

3. Peter Funk, *Funk and Wagnalls Standard College Dictionary* (Funk and Wagnalls, 1977), s.v. "communion."

4. As quoted in material advertising Kathryn Kuhlman's *I Believe in Miracles* DVD series, Vol. 16, "The Holy Spirit," accessed January 18, 2012, http://www.impactchristianbooks.com/Products.aspx?GroupMedia=4&Cat=14.

5. Hayford, ed., *Spirit-Filled Life Bible*, "Word Wealth" commentary for Ezekiel 3.

CHAPTER 6

BECOMING THE MESSAGE

"You shall speak My words to them, whether they hear or whether they refuse, for they are rebellious. But you, son of man, hear what I say to you. Do not be rebellious like that rebellious house; open your mouth and eat what I give you." Now when I looked, there was a hand stretched out to me; and behold, a scroll of a book was in it. Then He spread it before me; and there was writing on the inside and on the outside, and written on it were lamentations and mourning and woe. Moreover He said to me, "Son of man, eat what you find; eat this scroll, and go, speak to the house of Israel." So I opened my mouth, and He caused me to eat that scroll. (Ezekiel 2:7–3:2)

GOD told Ezekiel to eat the message (scroll) that He would to give to him. Before the prophet could effectively relay the message to the rebellious children of Israel, it was absolutely vital that he ingest it first. The message had to become part of who he was. When a message is a part of you and not just floating around in your mind, it drives you, motivates you, and moves you to action. It holds weight and power and touches everything around you. People of vision are people with a message, and that message always produces fruit—either good or bad depending on its source. It is not the heart of God for you to just know things in your mind. You could have a lot of knowledge, but what concerns God the most is that knowledge translating into an experience in your life. What are you doing with what you know?

John 6:63-64 says:

> *It is the Spirit who gives life; the flesh profits nothing. The words that I* [Jesus] *speak to you are spirit, and they are life. But there are some of you who do not believe*. . . .

Jesus' words weren't just the mere words of a man; they were spirit and life to the hearers because of where they came from. Why? Jesus was the very message He was speaking. He wasn't spewing out information out of His mind; He was releasing words that came from who He was and not just what He knew. When you have experienced something in your life, you have the authority and right to reproduce that same life in somebody else. You cannot reproduce something you don't have in someone else. If you want to see people walk in healing yet you've never seen or experienced healing in your own life, how can you reproduce that revelation in someone else? Revelation must become an experience in your own life before you can see it multiplied in someone's else's life. A seed is multiplied when it grows into what it is destined to be and produces other seeds. You can only reproduce what you have and who you are. Jesus said that His words are spirit and life. When Jesus spoke, He spoke out of the reality of who He was. He was the testimony, so that we could have a testimony. He was the walking Word. He was the

Word in flesh and embodied everything He ever preached (see John 1:14). Reproducing spiritual life in another is the most valuable thing a person can do in life, echoing throughout all eternity.

> *You can only reproduce*
> *what you have and who you are.*

There was something different about what Jesus said compared to what the religious teachers of the day said. They spoke out of their knowledge, whereas Jesus spoke out of who He was. He was the Word. He didn't just know the Word—He was and is the Word. You may have heard teachers or preachers who preach a good sermon or message, but if their preaching has not been ingested in their own lives, transforming them, then they will have a hard time, outside of the sovereignty of God, imparting that reality to you for the purpose of transformation. In some Jesus-believing circles, the Word (the Bible) is honored above the person of the Word Himself. Then everything becomes a mental assent rather than an experience of Jesus Himself. I have no doubt that many people could create a nice sermon with the words found in Scripture, and it may sound profound and really polished with three rhyming points and catchy Christian one-liners, but that does not mean there will be authority to reproduce life in people outside of God sovereignly taking your words and breathing life on them. A message can be misconstrued or not received because of the messenger. When the messenger has actually ingested the message, becoming the message itself, it's easier for the hearer to accept and experience it because of the authority when the messenger speaks.

And so it was, when Jesus had ended these sayings, that the people were astonished at His teaching, for He taught them as one having authority, and not as the scribes (Matthew 7:28-29).

Jesus was the message and that's why when He spoke it was with authority, not like the teachers of the law. He spoke out of who He was through what He possessed from the Father.

In John 7:46, we see this again. The officers said to the chief priests and Pharisees, *"No man ever spoke like this Man!"* In other words, there was an acknowledgment that something was truly different about this Jesus. God wants us to have the experiential knowledge of Him that exudes His authority and power. The Bible says that *"knowledge puffs up,"* or, as God's Word® Translation says, *"Knowledge makes people arrogant"* (I Cor. 8:1). You can fill your mind with all kinds of knowledge, but it won't do anything for you until it goes into your heart and transforms you. No longer is it just a thought or principle; it becomes a heart experience that drives you and moves you. The love that is experienced through Jesus then becomes your motivator, not knowledge or religious obligation.

The Pharisees, the religious teachers of the law in that time, had all kinds of knowledge and scriptural truth in their minds. They honored God with their lips, but their *hearts* were far away (see Mark 7:6). They knew their stuff and diligently studied the Scriptures, but they failed to see the very person the prophets had prophesied about standing right in front of them. I know people who memorize Scripture, who know Scripture; but there's no transformation in their lives. They don't even know what much of it means. They just memorize for the sake of memorizing. I am in no way downplaying the importance of memorizing scripture, just as long as we understand that the true intended purpose is for transformation.

In John 5:39-40, Jesus rebukes the religious, saying:

> *You search the Scriptures, for in them you think you have eternal life;*
> *and these are they which testify of Me. But you are not willing to*
> *come to Me that you may have life.*

They put all their focus on the word only and missed the Word in flesh standing before them.

I hold that a true sign of the power of Scripture in someone's life is transformation and an illumination of purpose and destiny. The Word of God is a light to help us see clearer. Psalm 119:105 says it lights up our present situation and illuminates where we are to go next: *"Your word is a lamp to my feet and a light to my path."*

Holy Spirit makes the Word life to us. God wants us to become the walking revelation of Christ on earth. You are a gateway to Heaven because Christ is in you, and He was the gateway to Heaven. Just like Him, you are called to be the walking Word in the flesh as His representative on the earth. Someone else can encounter Jesus through you because of who you are—a son or daughter of God Almighty. As you understand the importance of becoming the message, you will see people transformed around you. God wants you to be the living example of what you want to see reproduced in your spouse, children, friends, and family. You are called to be the living example of the Word. Having just biblical knowledge won't give you spiritual authority and power. Knowing Him and experiencing Him who is the source of it all, though, will. This is why someone's testimony is so powerful and authoritative. You can't argue with a testimony. It carries life.

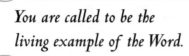

*You are called to be the
living example of the Word.*

DECREEING WORDS OF LIFE

Words carry the power of life when spoken because His life and power are within us. When we speak what God speaks, it is no longer from a knowledge-based faith or understanding, but from a heart transformation. As a result, our words begin to initiate change in the atmosphere around us. This is why becoming the very message that you believe is so important. My wife and I have tried to model this in our lives ever since we got married. We didn't follow the pattern that most people do who get married. We didn't have all our ducks lined up in a row. In fact, most people around us thought we were being irresponsible, or, at least, that I was being irresponsible. We moved six times in the first year after we were married. Our first bed was an air mattress, and we didn't own any furniture. We had no monetary or physical security, no house, and no long-term place to stay. Through this season, we, as a couple, learned to lean on God for our provision and all that we needed. We let Holy Spirit help us build a foundation of faith where we actually learned to call most of our needs in through prayer through the revelation of His sufficient provision available to us. The revelation of Jesus as our provider became a part of us; we really "ate the scroll" in that season of life.

We prayed and thanked God ahead of time for both of our cars. Two cars were given to us. When I needed a new computer, my wife felt strongly that I was to call the new computer in by faith in prayer and thanksgiving. For the next six months, I thanked God for what was to come, with all the specifications and details. Within six months, someone sent me a check for $3,000 to buy the exact laptop I was believing for. The list goes on with small and big things that we have had to believe for and called in through prayer and thanksgiving. This is the awesome faithfulness of God.

During times like this you find out what the Lord's heart is for you, making it easy to partner with Him through prayer and decree, thanking Him for what He wants to give to you. There's power in your prayers, never forget that. Your thankfulness for what is to come is a decree that agrees with Heaven's plan for your life. Don't just pray and decree something "hoping that one day maybe"; no, pray and declare knowing with full assurance that whatever He has already promised you have because of His Word.

So when we pray as led by the Spirit, we are coming into agreement with God. When we pray for someone's protection or safety, we are agreeing with Heaven's promise over us that we are to be protected and safe. Jesus is our intercessor, and He is praying for us. We are to co-labor with Him in prayer and in this journey, praying what He prays, doing what He does. God cares about every part of our lives. We are the New Covenant temples. Look back in the Old Testament at how God adorned the temple. It was so detailed and complex, yet so rich and extravagant. As living temples of the New Covenant of grace, how much more is God interested in adorning every detail of our life with His DNA and blessing? He cares about these simple realities. If you care, and your heart is pure in motive and aligned with the interests of the Kingdom, then rest assured, God cares too.

As a parent, you want to give whatever is beneficial and helpful to your children. How much more does God? You may think, *Why would God want to give me anything?* I'm not at all implying that believers should make a list of what they want and then spend all their days calling those things in prayer. People can get carried away and take certain principles of God out of context and to an extreme. I can usually tell when the things I'm praying for will happen and when certain things are just not for this season. I believe the Lord cares about it all, but He wants to know, "Why do you want what you want?" In the end, God knows your heart and will help you filter what's of Him and not of Him. Ask yourself questions like, *Is it selfish or is it Kingdom-focused? Am I considering James 4:3 that says, "You ask and do not receive, because you ask amiss, that you may spend it on your pleasures"? Why do I need this right now?* In the end, God is not looking at the thing that you're going after necessarily, but rather your heart motives during the process.

Right now you may be in desperate need of something. Begin to filter out why and the purpose behind whatever it is. If there is a peace from Holy Spirit, begin to pray and call it in. Decree it into your reality by simply thanking Him that it is available to you in Christ. With the Lord, time as we understand it does not exist. Sometimes things take seconds, minutes, hours, days, weeks, months, or even years when it comes to our requests to God. Don't give up even if you don't see something happen the first year you pray. My wife is amazing at praying for things and calling them in. The truth is, she sees it because she believes with a pure heart motive that God wants to give it to her. She prays for good deals when she goes shopping, and favor follows her, even to the extent where a woman she did not know walked up to her in the mall and gave her money to buy clothes. God is so good and amazing, and yes, God can even be a part of your shopping experience.

"You do not have because you do not ask" is a powerful truth found in James 4:2. And the reality of it is that God knows what you need before you even ask (see Matt. 6:8)—but He still loves hearing you ask for it. It's part of the intimate relationship we are called to with

our Creator. He loves to hear us talk even though He knows what we will ask before we do. He's a good Father, and He loves it when His children go to Him first. You may know your children want something by their actions and responses, but how much greater it is to hear them actually ask you so you can then respond by giving it to them. It's an amazing privilege as a parent to do this.

EATING THE FRUIT OF YOUR WORDS

Proverbs 18:21 says, *"Death and life are in the power of the tongue, and those who love it will eat its fruit."*

Years ago I was ministering at the Mardi Gras festival in New Orleans, and I received a phone call from one of my team members. The team thought they might have to call an ambulance for a woman who appeared to have alcohol poisoning. She was totally beside herself drunk and extremely sick from the alcohol. When we showed up, the woman was not in good shape, so we did what we could to help her. She was not only drunk, but she also had lost her cell phone, could not recall where her hotel was, and had been separated from her husband and friends—she was totally lost.

We felt the Lord say, "Prophesy over her." You may be wondering, *Why minister to someone who is all boozed up? She won't remember anything you say.* I believe that if led by Holy Spirit, ministering to a drunk person's spirit is no different from ministering to people who are sober and don't listen. Remember, if God authors it, His words will not return void. As mentioned previously, Ezekiel the prophet in the Old Testament was called by God to minister to a rebellious nation, as were Moses and so many others. God is faithful, and if He initiates it, it will produce fruit eventually. Besides, during the outreaches at Mardi

Gras, many times people who were completely drunk, sobered up in moments from one word from Jesus.

So we began to speak life and truth into her, relaying the heart and mind of the Father, but it seemed like she wasn't hearing us. We did this for quite some time, and in the natural, we saw no visible results. All the words of life we were speaking over her and her situation seemed to be bouncing back at us, yet we really felt this was what God wanted us to do. We ended up leaving that night without seeing any real change or visible sign that anything spiritual happened to her.

The rest of the story? Exactly one year later we were back again on the streets of Mardi Gras and in the same area where we had met this woman the year before. Guess who our team saw? This same woman! Only this time she was bringing the love and power of Jesus to the streets of Mardi Gras. We were told that one week after the encounter with our team the year prior, both she and her husband had an encounter with Jesus. They were totally transformed. Wow! God wanted to show us to never underestimate the power of our words. When authored by Him, anything can happen. We tasted Proverbs 18:21. We ate it! *"Death and life are in the power of the tongue, and those who love it will eat its fruit."* One year later, we got to eat the fruit of our tongues empowered by the Spirit. We love tasting the results of things we do in the Spirit; seeing a harvest come from the faith walk we are called to, is so rewarding. We don't always have to see immediate results. Results are a by-product of listening to Holy Spirit and acting on His word even if it takes a year or longer to see something happen.

When our words are authored by God, anything can happen.

USING THE TONGUE WISELY

And the tongue is a fire, a world of iniquity. The tongue is so set among our members that it defiles the whole body, and sets on fire the course of nature; and it is set on fire by hell (James 3:6).

Because our tongues are so powerful, there has been some abuse in many prophetic circles over the years. In the negative sense, James 3:6 says the tongue can set the whole person on fire when used incorrectly. On the flip side, we can have tongues of Holy Spirit fire, like those seen in Acts 2:3 during the outpouring of Holy Spirit, for the purpose of advancing the Kingdom and bringing life to the hopeless. Jeremiah 23:29 says, *"'Is not My word like a fire?' says the Lord, 'and like a hammer that* ✗ *breaks the rock in pieces?'"* His word in our mouth has such creative fiery power to break the hardest of situations and the hardest of hearts. All believers are guilty of saying words that are destructive and not encouraging. We need to be releasing words that build up people rather than tear them down.

Proverbs 12:18 says, *"There is one who speaks like the piercings of a sword, but the tongue of the wise promotes health."* And Proverbs 15:4 says, *"A wholesome tongue is a tree of life, but perverseness in it breaks the spirit."* For instance, simply saying the words, "Jesus loves you," can lead to someone being healed because they are powerful words from the heart of the Father. Proverbs 16:24 says, *"Pleasant words are like a honeycomb, sweetness to the soul and health to the bones."* The Hebrew word here for "pleasant" means delight, splendor or grace, or beauty.[1] And the word for "honeycomb" in Hebrew means to be overflowing, sticky, gummy, thick, and dripping.[2] When you speak a pleasant, delightful word full of grace and beauty to your spouse, daughter, son, friend, or parent, it has the power to stick to that individual and transform him or her. Such words bring sweetness and health, as the verse states.

HEART MOTIVES AND A CLEAR MIND

Life is in belief in Jesus, not in knowledge or words on a page. Clearly what you speak has a direct effect on the people around you. If you want to be a mouthpiece for God, learn to know His heart and mind and make sure your life is in right standing with Him (see John 3:3). The key to a sanctified mind is constantly allowing Holy Spirit to renew your thoughts and remind you that you have the mind of Christ. Let your true spiritual reality dictate your conditional, temporary reality on this earth. Your mind is a prophetic tool, and if your mind is polluted by garbage that you have allowed in, it can poison the words you speak. What you ingest will eventually come out. Let's ingest the good news of the finished work of the cross every day, then see what comes out of our mouths.

If you were to meditate on Jesus and the goodness of God for the next 12 hours, you would be radically affected in so many ways. Thinking is a form of meditation. Whatever is most occupying your thoughts, you are meditating on. If money is always on your mind, you are actually operating in a form of meditation by focusing your thoughts on money—thereby empowering greed and all kinds of evil. If it's fear and worry that occupy your mind space, then you are empowering fear and worry in your life through meditation. Paul said in Colossians 3 to keep your mind or thoughts fixed on things above where Christ is seated. Focus all of your attention on things above because, when you do, you will act differently. You will be different and talk differently.

Paul said to the church of the Thessalonians to pray without ceasing (see 1 Thess. 5:17). What does that mean? You could say that he wanted them to have Jesus on their mind all the time, which is actually a form of intimate communion. Paul wouldn't have given this charge to them if it wasn't a part of his own life (see Rom. 15:18)—even in his work, his tough times, and his travels. It's easy to be in constant communication with God when your thoughts are fixed on Him. What you think most about determines most of what comes out of your mouth.

Belief in the heart that is connected to confession with the mouth of the finished work of Jesus brings about the most significant transformation possible. Romans 10:9 says if you confess with your mouth that Jesus is Lord and believe with your heart that He was raised from the dead, you will be saved. It doesn't say if you confess with your mouth and believe in your mind, or if you believe in the principle of salvation or in good theology that your mind can comprehend. If your heart believes in something, your heart will always move you to action and to receive whatever is needed for transformation.

PROPHETIC IMPACT

Just like the prophets of old, there are things that you will declare that you may not necessarily see in your lifetime, but that will eventually happen and bring forth fruit (see Isa. 55:11). Although we love to see things happen right when we pray and hope that we'll see the answer while we are still living, by faith we trust in God that His perfect timing is always best. I have received emails years and years after giving people a word from God telling me what has happened as a result of what God told them through me a long time before.

One day before I was saved, I received a phone call from a friend of mine at one o'clock in the morning. I had been sitting in my basement with another friend watching a movie. I was at one of the lowest points in my life, and I was not yet a true believer in Jesus Christ. My best friend Caleb, who called me, had just had an encounter with God in his bedroom. At that point in my life I had no grid for the power of God—no idea what it looked like when God touched someone. All I heard was weeping from him on the phone. I thought he was having an asthma attack and was a little worried because he could barely get a word out.

Once he got himself together and began speaking coherently, he eventually told me that as he had been praying in his room, he had had this powerful encounter with God. He said, "It was like liquid fire came into my fingertips and to the rest of my body. I ended up on the floor shaking and weeping under the power of God." During this encounter, the Lord told him to call me. He fought it and fought it, but eventually went downstairs to the kitchen and called me. He began to speak things into my life that he had no way of knowing—it kind of freaked me out. That was the beginning, in many ways, of my journey to receive Jesus as Lord into my life, but it wasn't until months after that that I actually had a personal encounter with Jesus in my car while driving on the highway.

*God's words to us
always bring breakthrough.*

God's words to us and for situations always bring breakthrough. As alluded to earlier in this chapter, Jeremiah 23:29 says, *"'Is not My word like a fire?' says the Lord, 'and like a hammer that breaks a rock in pieces?'"* His words bring breakthrough. His words can change the hardest of situations. I remember being in the hospital prior to the birth of our first daughter, Promise. There were some complications that the doctors were quite worried about. When she finally came into this world, she wasn't crying, or even responsive. They rushed her to a table where eight to ten specialists worked on her. They said that they would have to rush her to ICU and that she would likely have pneumonia. Faith then rose up within me and, in front of all the doctors and nurses, I pushed my way in to see my daughter and declared over her, "In Jesus' name, you will not have pneumonia." I declared health over her. Then they rushed her to ICU and said that the family would not be able visit her for the time being, even though they had been waiting in the hospital for more than 24 hours. After explaining to our family what had happened, I went back to the ICU to see how she was doing. The nurses said to me, "We honestly don't know what happened, but your daughter is totally fine and can go back and see her mother now." The doctors were confounded. But my wife and I knew what happened. Never underestimate the power of your words. Decree with the leading of the Spirit and it will be established (see Job 22:28). This is the life of sons and daughters of God who are led of the Spirit in everything (see Rom. 8:14). Sons and daughters know their God and become the very message of faith and confidence in their Father.

THE STIRRING OF A WORD

When His word is declared over us, it begins the journey for us to become the very manifestation of that word. Joseph, the 11th child of

Jacob, is an example of this. He had a dream and soon after the course of his life was shaped and designed in reference to that word becoming a manifestation in his life.

The goal of the prophetic is to see people as God sees them, speaking into their destiny, potential, and treasure in their heart, pointing them to Christ and to who they are destined to be. When you prophesy over someone, declaring what God is speaking to you, it stirs up his or her spirit man, moving that person into his or her destiny.

The prophetic word noted in Judges 6:11-12 is another example of this. Gideon is hanging out one day, brushing his teeth, and an angel shows up and says to Gideon, *"The Lord is with you, you mighty man of valor!"* That's all the angel said. No big, long prophetic word full of intricate detail; just the simple reality that God was with him and the truth of what God saw in him. Gideon probably didn't believe that about himself. In fact, his very situation and circumstance at that time was totally contradictory to that word. He probably thought, *I don't feel like the Lord is with me, and I don't feel like a mighty man of valor.* Gideon was depressed and pretty down on himself—after all, he was hiding from the enemy in a winepress where he thought the Midianites would not find him. He was from the weakest clan in Manasseh and the least in his father's house (see Judg. 6:15), and he doubted the word spoken over his life by the angel.

But God spoke into Gideon's potential and purpose, releasing the reality of his destiny. The fruit of the word is found in Judges 8:28. Gideon became the mighty man of valor he was destined to become; he was a mighty deliverer in the land. In Hebrews 11:32, Gideon is mentioned as a mighty hero. He had a powerful influence in the end, but in the beginning he was the lowest of the low. One word from God set in motion a series of events that brought him into his destiny and purpose, allowing him to become the message of victory and faith in his God.

We see this reality of stirring again in Haggai 1:13: *"Then Haggai, the Lord's messenger, spoke the Lord's message to the people, saying, 'I am with you, says the Lord.'"* A simple message, but what was the result?

> *So the Lord **stirred** up the spirit of Zerubbabel the son of Shealtiel, governor of Judah, and the spirit of Joshua the son of Jehozadak, the high priest, and the spirit of all the remnant of the people; and they came and worked on the house of the Lord of hosts, their God* (Haggai 1:14).

The word reunited and reawakened the people with vision to rebuild the temple that had been lying in shambles. Before this word from Haggai, they had made some progress, but were discouraged and stopped. The prophetic word from Haggai the prophet stirred them up to action again. Their spirits were aroused and awakened to purpose and destiny with one word from God.

When Holy Spirit communicates with you, He touches your spirit. Remember, you are a spiritual being in a human body. That's what you are. You're not a human body with a spirit, but a spirit with a human earth suit. You first existed in God before the foundation of the world in spirit, but not yet in physical flesh form (see Eph. 1:4). The Hebrew word for "stirred" is *ur*, meaning to arouse, awaken, stir up, raise up, or arouse to action.[3] My favorite definition of *ur* is to open one's eyes.[4] When God speaks to you, your eyes are opened in a new way to see a whole new side of God and of your life and calling that you have never seen before. This word *ur* is also used when an eagle stirs up its nest, as in Deuteronomy 32:11:

> *As an eagle **stirs** up its nest, hovers over its young, spreading out its wings, taking them up, carrying them on its wings.*

When the prophetic word comes, it stirs up those the word comes into contact with and gets them ready for a new journey of life. When God speaks, it nourishes and causes us to fly with Him above all the problems and issues of life, bringing hope and directives and releasing confidence for the journey ahead. God doesn't want us to stay in the nest of mediocrity and comfort. He wants us to get out of the nest and fly, move, and co-labor with Him because we are co-heirs. The eagle is a symbol of the prophetic in Scripture. We see it again in Revelation 12:14, which speaks of the witnessing end-time church:

> *But the woman was given two wings of a great eagle, that she might fly into the wilderness to her place, where she is nourished for a time and times and half a time, from the presence of the serpent.*

Without going into a theological stance on my eschatology, I want to highlight the connection between the eagle's wings and strength, encouragement, and comfort from the enemy for the woman. First Corinthians 14:3 states that the prophetic is for encouragement, strength, and comfort. We see the eagle connection again in Exodus 19:4 when God is talking to Israel about how He protected them and carried them on eagles' wings to Himself. It speaks of protection and deliverance from bondage.

EATING HIS WORDS

Jesus says in John 4:34, *"My food is to do the will of Him who sent Me, and to finish His work."* How did Jesus fulfill the will of God on the earth? The answer is found in John 5:19-20, where Jesus is addressing the nonbelieving crowd:

*Then Jesus answered and said to them, "Most assuredly, I say to you, the Son can do nothing of Himself, **but what He sees the Father do**; for whatever He does, the Son also does in like manner. For the Father loves the Son, and shows Him all things that He Himself does; and He will show Him greater works than these, that you may marvel.*

Jesus is the prototype we are to follow as sons and daughters adopted and grafted into the family of the Kingdom.

He could fulfill the Father's will on the earth by learning to do and say only what He saw and heard the Father say, in full surrender. What nourished Him and kept Him going was fulfilling His destiny, fueled by the directives from His Father as the spiritual food to empower Him for great supernatural works. As Christians—meaning little Christs—this is the prototype we are to follow as sons and daughters adopted and grafted into the family of the Kingdom. We are co-heirs with Him, having divine privileges and access to the Creator Himself (see Heb. 4:16; Rom. 8:17). Jesus relates again to the communication of the Father to Him while in the wilderness temptations with the devil. Matthew 4:1-4 states:

Then Jesus was led up by the Spirit into the wilderness to be tempted by the devil. And when He had fasted forty days and forty nights, afterward He was hungry. Now when the tempter came to Him, he said, "If You are the Son of God, command that these stones become bread." But He answered and said, "It is written, 'Man shall not live by bread alone, but by every word that proceeds from the mouth of God.'"

Many people interpret Jesus' response to the devil's first temptation to mean that in order to fight against the devil, we use the *logos* word, the written letter of the Bible. Although the Scripture is a great weapon, a double-edged sword as Hebrews 4:12 states, this is not what Jesus actually meant. The Greek word for "word" here is *rhema*, which is known as communication directly from the Father. Jesus was actually quoting a scripture found in Deuteronomy 8:3:

So He humbled you, allowed you to hunger, and fed you with manna which you did not know nor did your fathers know, that He might make you know that man shall not live by bread alone; but man lives by every word that proceeds from the mouth of the Lord.

Earthly provisions of food, clothing, and such are not, in the end, what we need the most. We need His spiritual nourishment that comes through walking out the promises declared by His very mouth, trusting in Him for everything and hearing and recognizing His voice.

As New Covenant believers, we are destined to live for real relationship with Jesus Christ. It's a relationship full of communication by both sides. When He speaks to us, it's nourishment and strength for us to walk into everything He has promised us. We say so often that we are what we eat. So when you feed on the person of Jesus and His finished work of the cross, you become the very reflection of that reality and truth. His word to us and over us transforms us to a place where we become the very manifestation of the word.

HEALING WORDS

When you truly believe something in your heart, the words that you speak regarding it have the potential to carry life or death, changing a situation or circumstance as we have mentioned earlier. For a short time years ago I lived in Alaska, where I had been leading some street outreach. During one of these outreaches we had planned to go into a local hospital to pray for the sick. Before we left for the hospital, I prayed and asked God to bring me into a vision of what was going to happen in the hospital. I soon saw myself in a room looking at a heavy-set woman in a hospital bed. She had short hair and looked to be in her late 60s. God began to speak to me about her legs and her back, and about the depression and suicide in her life. He said that four years ago something traumatic had happened to her, that had opened the door to the sickness she was experiencing at the present time. There were other details that I wrote down so I wouldn't forget. (I advise everyone who receives words of knowledge from the Lord to write them down. It can be so easy to forget.)

When we reached the hospital, we visited a few rooms, and then walked into a room where an older woman with short hair was lying in a bed. Sitting next to her was her daughter. We were told that there was no hope for this woman; death was looming. When we asked her daughter some questions, she told us that not only were there problems in her mother's legs and back, but she also had a variety of other life-threatening ailments. Some of her organs were diseased, and her body was shutting down.

She was not a believer in Jesus, nor was her daughter. We began to worship and pray right there in the room. The atmosphere began to change and the woman in the bed began to cry as she could tangibly sense the presence of someone powerful in the room—Jesus. As I placed my hand on her, I prayed the vision that I had seen prior to coming to the hospital. As I said, "And, Father, four years ago something traumatic happened to her and..." her daughter immediately stopped me mid-prayer and asked, "How do you know about four years ago?"

I shared with her how Jesus is real and He speaks today—that He had shown me her mother in a vision before coming to the hospital. She said that four years ago, her father—the sick woman's husband—had died and since that time she had been sick and almost bedridden. The daughter was quite amazed and touched in her spirit to think that a loving God would reveal this kind of information. We continued to minister to her mother, yet we didn't really see any visible signs of change. The moment we left the room, she began to violently vomit. Her daughter came rushing out after us, certain that we caused the reaction. One of the women in our group went back into the woman's room and whispered in her ear, "This is the Lord delivering and healing you. Let it happen." Even though we didn't see a visible sign of healing at that time, we knew Jesus had done something.

One week later, part of our team returned to the hospital to check on her and found that she had been released from the hospital—totally healed in her body. So you see it doesn't matter how specific or how powerful you may think your word is, when it's from God, it has the power to change and alter the course of people's lives, not only in their future and destiny, but in their physical bodies as well.

THE IMPORTANCE OF WHO WE KNOW

There's a deception in our society today that says it's all about what we know. But in reality, it's all about who we know. You become like those you hang out with the most. What you behold and engage with, you become. That's why Paul encourages us to keep our minds fixed on things above. Often opportunities come because of who you know. Our society, though, projects the demand on all of us to attain knowledge (don't get me wrong, knowledge is good).

It was said of those who turned the world upside down because of this gospel message in Acts 4 that they were unschooled, untrained fishermen with no education, but that they had been with Jesus. The disciples knew Him by experience, not just as someone written about in a book. Their skill or lack of skill did not determine their life call or future. The extent of their impact on society was determined by their relationship with Jesus. I'm not saying that you don't need training to become a brain surgeon or a teacher. Obviously, I would not want a brain surgeon with no training to operate on my brain, or a school-teacher with no education to teach my children. But I believe Jesus needs to be our priority in everything we do.

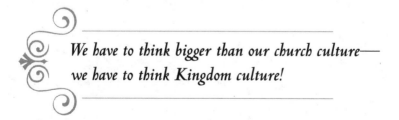

We have to think bigger than our church culture—
we have to think Kingdom culture!

Follow the leading of the Spirit, and let education be an addition to the equation, not the solution. Christ needs to be in the beginning and end of every decision, moving you into becoming the message of experiencing supernatural life.

ENDNOTES

1. Strong, *The New Strong's Exhaustive Concordance of the Bible*, #H5277, #H5276.

2. Ibid., #H6688, #H1706.

3. Ibid., #H5781.

4. Hayford, ed., *Spirit-Filled Life Bible*, "Word Wealth" commentary for Haggai 1.

CHAPTER 7

UNDERSTANDING THE
LANGUAGE OF THE SPIRIT

*As for these four young men, God gave them knowledge and skill
in all literature and wisdom; and Daniel had understanding
in all visions and dreams.* (Daniel 1:17)

G OD speaks to all five of our senses—taste, smell, hearing, touch, and sight. He wants to awaken our senses and knock down the barriers that have stopped us or limited us from hearing, interpreting, and discerning His voice.

Many people box themselves in and make statements like, "This is the only way God speaks to me." Some like to play biblical roulette by opening the Bible randomly to see what it says. Others say it's only in the still, small voice or through feelings and impressions that God will speak to them.

Although these are all valid, they aren't the only methods of communication from God. It's easy to become comfortable with the way He usually speaks to us. But in the midst of our comfort and security, we may miss other opportunities and potential experiences because of a lack of awareness and understanding. There are many different ways that God speaks and tries to get our attention.

Genesis 28:16 says, *"Then Jacob awoke from his sleep and said, 'Surely the Lord is in this place, and I did not know it.'"*

It's not uncommon to find yourself in an environment where there is clearly a move of the supernatural power of God and to see with your eyes what is happening, but at the same time not really see, spiritually speaking. Or to hear what's going on, but not really hear. It's almost like a veil of dullness sets in over our spiritual senses and, like Jacob, we don't even realize it until later. Jesus spoke about this reality in the Gospel of Mark when the disciples were asking Him about the meaning of the parable of the sower:

> *But when He was alone, those around Him with the twelve asked Him about the parable. And He said to them, "To you it has been given to know the mystery of the kingdom of God; but to those who are **outside**, all things come in parables, so that 'Seeing they may see and not perceive, and hearing they may hear and not understand; lest they should turn, and their sins be forgiven them'"* (Mark 4:10-12; see Isaiah 6:9-10).

As a believer in Christ, if your entire focus is on the external works of Christianity, you are missing the point of the finished work of the cross. Your spiritual senses will be dulled as long as you are seeking to fill your life with just the works of Christianity. Faith in Jesus and what He has done for you is the key. What you do will be a sweet overflow of that revelation and belief. You and I need to live from the inside out by a right revelation of Jesus Christ and His finished work. This will illuminate our senses and increase our sensitivity to His love and presence in our lives.

> *Faith in Jesus and what He has done for you is the key. What you do will be a sweet overflow of that revelation and belief.*

SPIRITUAL DIGGING

I hear people say all the time, "I had a dream last night, but I don't understand it. If it is of God, God will show me what it means." That is not wisdom or at all a biblical approach. Proverbs 25:2 says, *"It is the glory of God to conceal a matter, but the glory of kings is to search out a matter."* In the Old Testament we see even the nonbelievers so valued their dreams that they surrounded themselves with all sorts of spiritual counsel. Sure, those counselors may have been soothsayers, mediums, astrologers, and magicians, but they held dreams in high value and of great importance. Dreams weren't so easily passed off as nothing—as they seem to be today in both the church and secular cultures.

Look at King Nebuchadnezzar. He surrounded himself with astrologers, magicians, and various spiritual counsels for the purpose of wisdom and insight when he did not have it. Then the king appointed Daniel, a believer in God Almighty, and his three friends to leadership concerning all spiritual matters. Daniel continued for more than 60 years in this area of responsibility. Daniel 1:17-20 says:

As for these four young men, God gave them knowledge and skill in all literature and wisdom; and Daniel had understanding in all visions and dreams. Now at the end of the days, when the king had said that they should be brought in, the chief of the eunuchs brought them in before Nebuchadnezzar. Then the king interviewed them, and among them all none was found like Daniel, Hananiah, Mishael, and Azariah; therefore they served before the king. And in all matters of wisdom and understanding about which the king examined them, he found them ten times better than all the magicians and astrologers who were in all his realm.

If a king, who did not know the Creator as Daniel did, understood the value of what seemed to be unknown enigmas, dreams, and visions, how much more do we as believers in Jesus Christ who have a 24-hour-a-day relationship with Him need to seek out understanding from Him? When God is vague about things, the majority of the time it's so you will draw close to Him with your affections and focus, searching for wisdom and understanding. It's in the process of the search that we come into a greater encounter with His goodness, glory, and revelation of Jesus in our lives.

God wants to woo you into a deeper understanding of His loving nature and establish in you a stable relationship with Him so you are no longer tossed around because of spiritual immaturity. He wants the mystery, the unknown, to draw you into a search with the purpose of getting to know His ways. Jesus' parables did just this. They were for the hungry. They sorted out the fertile from the wayside soil. The word *parable* means "a casting alongside." A parable is like a treasure map thrown onto the ground, pointing to a mystery and secret treasure.[1] But the only way to discover the treasure is to pick up the map for yourself and begin to search. In Mark 4:10, we see the disciples grasped this concept of seeking out the treasure found in the person of Christ: *"But when He was alone, those around Him with the twelve asked Him about the parable."* Jesus would speak a parable, a natural illustration to relay a revelatory truth, and then behind the scenes the disciples would seek the meaning from Jesus Christ Himself. In Jesus are hidden all the treasures of wisdom and knowledge (see Col. 2:3). All hidden truths are found in the person of Jesus who is the door to the fullness of Heaven.

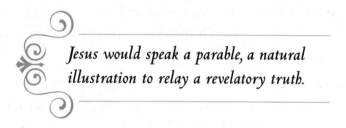

Jesus would speak a parable, a natural illustration to relay a revelatory truth.

You may have had a dream, vision, or spiritual experience you don't understand and it may be the wackiest, craziest experience ever. Don't pass it off without bringing it to the Lord. When speaking of dreams specifically, some of my wackiest, most incomprehensible dreams are the most powerful and most instrumental God-dreams I have ever had. I never pass any dream off immediately just because I don't understand it. Every time you flippantly pass off a dream saying it was just the food you ate the night before, you potentially devalue His voice to you. What you value in life you make room for, establishing accelerated growth and increase. We show value by digging into what could be His voice speaking.

PERCEIVING THE WAY OF COMMUNICATION

Job 33:14-16 says:

> *For God may speak in one way, or in another, yet man does not perceive it. In a dream, in a vision of the night, when deep sleep falls upon men, while slumbering on their beds, then He opens the ears of men, and seals their instruction.*

God may speak to you in a dream or in a vision of the night while you are sleeping; He may open your ears while you are sleeping, but yet you may not perceive His voice. It is important to learn to recognize God's voice and perceive it correctly.

God wants to communicate with you through all five of your senses. You're not learning to hear—you're already hearing. And you may already be seeing into the invisible. You are already feeling and tasting. You just don't recognize that God is reaching out to you through your senses yet. Like the scripture says, you could be hearing but not really hearing, seeing but not really seeing (see Matt. 13:13). For instance, if you walked into a room and all of a sudden had the taste of honey in your mouth, would you recognize it as God speaking to you through your taste buds? Do you believe God would speak to you through this way (see Rev. 10:9; Ezek. 3:3)?

If we don't have a biblical grid for these kinds of experiences, we end up trying to pass them off with some natural explanation, possibly thinking things like, "A few days ago I had honey in my coffee, and the taste is just coming back to me now." Without understanding and wisdom in matters concerning the supernatural communication of Heaven, we miss much of what He has for us. It's in God's heart and intentions to awaken our senses to His language and voice.

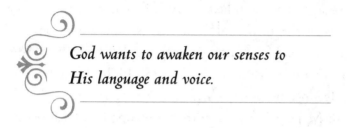

> *God wants to awaken our senses to*
> *His language and voice.*

This way of thinking is elementary for some, yet it's way out there for so many others. You may walk into a room and all of a sudden your knee begins to hurt and it never hurt before. Could it be that God is communicating to you through your body? Sometimes to communicate to your spirit, God may get your attention by awakening your physical senses. Often this is how a word of knowledge emerges. You begin to feel what the people around you are feeling, and it is God's way of giving you divine knowledge about someone's physical condition for the purpose of healing.

I remember a situation years ago when a few of us went to a downtown mall in Ottawa, Ontario, to demonstrate the love and power of Jesus. One person in our group was walking through the mall when all of a sudden she stopped and said she could feel pain in her knee. Immediately I knew it wasn't her pain, but a word of knowledge for someone around us in the mall. I looked over and saw a group of tough-looking dudes and one girl. I went over and asked each one, "Do you have something wrong with your knee?" Every one of them said no until I got to the last person who was a young woman in her 20s. She said yes, she had pain in her knee and foot and had a metal rod in her leg as a result of surgery. She walked with lots of pain, but when we prayed for her she was totally healed and experienced the reality of Jesus Christ in her life and gave her life to Him. As a result of her healing and accepting Jesus, another person in that group who had a stomach condition was healed as well. He also had an encounter with the reality of Jesus Christ and surrendered his life to Him. People had encounters with Jesus that night because we paid attention to the voice and direction of Holy Spirit by being sensitive to a feeling in someone's physical body in the group that was with us. In Mark 5 Jesus knew that someone had faith because He felt virtue leave His physical body even though everyone around Him was grabbing Him. One woman who had faith for her healing knew that if she could just touch His clothes, she would be healed. A spiritual reality transpired that affected what He felt in His physical body, causing Him to ask who touched Him (see Mark 5:25-34). In that moment He discerned something going on in the spiritual realm within Him, and it was communicated through what He felt in His physical body.

Always pay attention to random feelings and things that seem abnormal when you are in an environment with other people—you never know when it could be the Lord trying to get your attention about someone or something. Learning this way of communication is the same as learning to ride a bike. We become more comfortable as we keep on trying, even though we may make some mistakes and stumble along the way.

You may walk into a room and all of a sudden feel very anxious. You know there's no reason you should feel anxious, but you do. This could be a word of knowledge for someone who is dealing with anxiety—and you are the instrument chosen to encourage this person in the midst of his or her anxiety. If you don't learn to discern the importance of understanding your senses in God, then you'll probably just pass it off thinking, *Wow, I'm struggling with anxiety right now. I don't know why I feel so depressed. I never get depressed.* Don't be afraid to ask the Lord what He is doing.

Or maybe you walk into a room and all of a sudden you feel an overwhelming sense of compassion for an individual sitting in the corner. It's not just because you're a loving person; God wants to speak to you, and you are feeling His compassion. Jesus was moved with compassion, and as born-again believers in Him we are united with Him in every way.

Remember, chances are you *are* hearing and having these things happen to you, but you're not always perceiving or recognizing it is your heavenly Father communicating with you. Someone told me one time that I shouldn't use this Job 33 Scripture reference because all the friends of Job gave him bad advice. But that's not true. Elihu, the youngest of Job's four friends, is speaking in this passage, and he gave Job true godly counsel and wisdom. Elihu was saying that we don't always perceive or understand when God is speaking. Our awareness and sensitivity to the various ways God speaks must increase in this hour in the Body of Christ.

There are different interpretations of Job 33:14-16. I believe there are things that God will deposit in us in the night season that He does not allow us to remember for specific reasons; in other words, they are not always disclosed to us. It's like He seals them in the envelope of our spirit. I am sure that there are times when you know you have had a significant dream, but you can't recall it the next morning. You try and think back to the pieces of the dream you do remember, but you just can't seem to get it all. Or maybe you have nothing at all, but know you had a significant dream or experience in the night. Although there is a contextual explanation for the meaning of this scripture in Job 33, something that has always jumped out at me is the part that says, *"when deep sleep falls upon men, while slumbering on their beds, then He opens the ears of men and seals their instruction."* He seals our instruction in the night.

I can remember times, and I'm sure you can too, when I have been somewhere or with someone in a specific situation, and all of a sudden I realize that I have seen, or done, this or that before. Let me tell you that it sure didn't happen in another lifetime or as some sort of reincarnated creature. It most likely happened already in a dream. And in that very moment, the seal on the envelope of your spirit where that dream was deposited opened up to you. The classic label for this kind of experience is *déjà vu*, meaning already seen, having a sense that you have already witnessed or experienced a certain situation. When this experience happens to me, my first response is, "God, what are You doing?" I begin to inquire of the Lord for insight and understanding into the reason why I feel like I have been here and done this before. Often it can be a confirmation of the important reality that there is something significant about this situation; sometimes you need to lean into Holy Spirit and ask Him to show you what you are to do.

Some very pivotal moments and transitional seasons in my spiritual journey have been marked with these types of experiences. I believe they are there to get my attention about something important He wants to do in and through me in that particular time. Pay attention in these moments. You don't have to call it déjà vu if that makes you uncomfortable, but most understand that kind of language and can relate to it.

THE WRITTEN WORD OF GOD

Most believers in Christ focus on the Word as God's preferred method of communication because it seems to be the most comfortably received. Neither do they need a lot of faith to believe He can speak through His *logos* word—the Bible. As mentioned earlier in this chapter, many play the game of biblical roulette, opening the Bible and hoping words from the page jump out at them. Or when they are seeking God for an answer, they may open their Bibles and close their eyes while pointing at a scripture hoping it will be a now-word for them. Don't get me wrong, God does and can do this, but we simply cannot rely on this method as the only way of hearing Him speak to us. There are so many other ways He can and does speak. When He does speak this way, God has taken the *logos* word (the written Word) and turned it into a *rhema* word, which is the now-communication of that word.

Hebrews 4:12 says:

> *For the word of God is living and powerful, and sharper than any two-edged sword, piercing even to the division of soul and spirit, and of joints and marrow, and is a discerner of the thoughts and intents of the heart.*

The Greek word for "word" here is *logos*, meaning the written letter of the Word of God. This is different from the *rhema* word, which is the now spoken word communicated to the hearer. Some scholars and theologians say those words are synonymous, that they are connected or intertwined. But the fundamental foundation of the Greek word *rhema* is the communication of the word, whereas *logos* is the communication of the word through the written letter of the word. Holy Spirit speaks to us through His Word, and He can make the *logos* turn into a *rhema* in our lives. Years ago I was in a season in my life when I was about to transition to the United States from Canada. I felt God had spoken to me that I was to associate myself with and serve a ministry from the United States. I remember this step was a very big one for that time of my life, but so much had happened that I could not ignore it. That day I said to God these exact words: "God, I don't understand what You are doing." Seconds later, I opened the Bible to John 13:7. It wasn't highlighted or anything, but it jumped out off the page at me and totally blew my mind because of what I had just said to God seconds earlier: *"Jesus replied, 'You do not realize now what I am doing, but later you will understand'"* (John 13:7 NIV).

Now this kind of thing does not happen every day, and I believe it was because I was a fairly new believer that I needed it to happen that way. I wasn't necessarily looking at Scripture for an answer to my statement to God, but I was open to receiving from Him. The written Word was so closely related to what I had just said that it could not be ignored. If I looked at the context of that scripture, I could have gotten all analytical and thought, *Well, that really doesn't make sense if I read the whole passage in context.* But in that moment, that was what I needed to hear. God showed me that specific verse. This is a prime example of the *logos* word becoming a *rhema* word to you in a moment. Just don't expect to live there all the time.

Second Corinthians 3:6 says that *"the letter kills, but the Spirit gives life."* So the letter (the written Word) in itself without the Spirit guiding and teaching us, will not be life to us. Holy Spirit gives the Bible life. And the Bible is our sword that divides soul and spirit; it's a discerner, a lamp and light that illuminates our path and life.

With Holy Spirit's help, one of our greatest tools for measuring what comes from the Lord is knowing the Scriptures. You may have a dream, a vision, or some other channel of communication, and the best aid to interpreting and weighing its validity is knowing the written Word of God. For example, if you think God told you to sacrifice an animal to atone for your sin, then by understanding what Jesus did on the cross and knowing the Scriptures that testify of Jesus both in the Old and New Testaments, you would know that sacrificing an animal in the New Covenant is not from the Lord. We are in a New Covenant, and Jesus made the one-time, ultimate sacrifice atoning for the sin of humankind once and for all. We make the choice to accept or reject His sacrifice. No longer can we sacrifice anything to atone for our sin. He did it for us; a Man who knew no sin became sin for us (see 2 Cor. 5:21). He became our substitute, our sacrificial Lamb, not speaking of lamb chops but of Jesus pictured as the lamb that was slain for our freedom from sin and death.

We need the Word of God to help illuminate our hearts and minds when making decisions that we think are God's will. Sometimes people say they have heard from the Lord, but what they have are really thoughts born out of their own biases, hurts, and pain. This may happen because they have had to deal with unpleasant things in the past, and those memories trigger unhealthy thoughts and fears, which then infect what comes out of their mouths.

On many occasions people have approached me crying under what they think is the conviction of God, saying that God told them to ask for my forgiveness because they had judged me for the way I look (back when I had long dreadlocks). My first response has usually been, "God did not tell you that, because up until now I was fine." Telling someone who has no knowledge of your bitterness, jealousy, envy, judgments, etc. and asking for forgiveness is truly not honoring to God—because you are not honoring the individual. Without knowing this, you put the person in a very awkward position. These kinds of issues need to be dealt with in private with the Lord.

Just imagine if, every time you had a bad feeling or thought toward someone, you had to ask that person for forgiveness? Sooner or later that person might be in bad shape, especially if you're close to him or her. The Word of God needs to be our measuring stick for what we feel God is saying to us.

In Matthew 18:15 Jesus is speaking to His disciples:

> *Moreover if your brother sins against you, go and tell him his fault between you and him alone. If he hears you, you have gained your brother.*

Notice it says *"if your brother sins against you,"* not you in your heart sinning toward your brother when he is unaware of it. So here in Matthew 18 the instruction is flipped compared to my previous story. The person who has been sinned against is the one who looks to restore. This is not to say that the other person shouldn't look for forgiveness and restoration as well, but here the onus is on the one who has been wronged. We believers need to go back to a biblical paradigm for restoration and forgiveness; over and over again the emphasis is on how we must forgive others. The mature in Christ will always look for restoration and reconciliation in any situation.

True honor is to run toward conflict for resolution. Dishonor is to run from conflict, promoting division and strife. Make sure if you are seeking to be forgiven by someone for what you have done, that the person knows you have sinned against him or her. This is why we need to know the written Word of God.

> *True honor is to run toward conflict for resolution. Dishonor is to run from conflict, promoting division and strife.*

VISIONS

> *And **a vision appeared to Paul** in the night. A man of Macedonia stood and pleaded with him, saying, "Come over to Macedonia and help us." Now after he had seen the vision, **immediately** we sought to go to Macedonia, concluding that the Lord had called us to preach the gospel to them* (Acts 16:9-10).

Paul had trained his spiritual eyes and senses enough to discern whether something was of God or not. I love how it says here in Acts 16 that *"immediately"* they sought to go to Macedonia. Paul didn't say, "God, give me another confirmation, or a few fleeces and an angel." No. It was an immediate response to the word of the Lord. After encountering Jesus and walking in relationship with Him, we don't really need a confirmation to go and preach the gospel; that's an obvious next step. We know that message is from God. The devil is not out to encourage us to do the very thing that ruins his evil, inferior kingdom. So in this case, it was easy for Paul to discern the Giver of the vision.

The current reality of many believers is that they need confirmation for everything. People have even said to me, "Shawn, I felt God say to me that I was to tell the employee at the cash register that Jesus loves her, but I need a confirmation first." My response: "You don't need a confirmation; you just need to do it!" Remember, the devil has no encouraging words to say—especially about the love of Jesus. We need to stop complicating the words we hear from God and love people with the love of Jesus. There are times when you have to trust and step out. If you know the Scriptures, you will begin to know the heart of God, and that will help you respond to those spiritual promptings.

> *We need to stop complicating the words we hear from God and love people with the love of Jesus.*

Numbers 12:6 says, *"Hear now My words: If there is a prophet among you, I, the Lord, make Myself known to him in a vision; I speak to him in a dream."* Visions did not stop with the prophets of old, nor did they stop with the New Testament—all the more reason why visions remain a predominant way God may speak to His people today. God didn't just decide one day to change the way He had been speaking after thousands of years of communicating in these ways. God inspired His Word through the hands of men (see 2 Tim. 3:16) to give us a spiritual grid of expectation for what could be in the life of the believer in Christ.

You may have a vision with your eyes open or in your mind's eye in the realm of your imagination with your eyes closed. The devil did not give you an imagination—God did. In fact, the devil did not give you any part of your beautiful created body and nature. It's Spirit to spirit communication (see Rom. 8:16). Holy Spirit can grab your attention with one of your senses, but only to communicate to your spirit.

*But there is a God in heaven who reveals secrets, and He has made known to King Nebuchadnezzar what will be in the latter days. Your dream, and the **visions** of your head upon your bed, were these* (Daniel 2:28).

*I, Daniel, was grieved in my spirit within my body, and the **visions** of my head troubled me* (Daniel 7:15).

Barnes' *Notes on the Bible* says, "The head is here regarded as the seat of the intellect, and he speaks of these visions as if they were seen by the head. That is, they seemed to pass before his eyes."[2] In the Spirit you can see with your eyes closed and open. God can put a vision into the realm of your imagination, your mind's eye. I'm not calling this the third eye; rather, think of this as a spiritual visionary compartment that the Lord opens to you and me in His communication with us. Not that you're conjuring it up or imagining it, but since God uses all your faculties to speak to you, He'll put a vision in the realm of your imagination. Closed-eye visions don't have to be super wild or crazy spiritual. I know from experience that sometimes they are just as simple as a thought or a still image in your mind that comes while you are in prayer or engaging in normal everyday chores.

With your eyes open, God may say, "What do you see?" You may be staring at a door and that door is closed. Maybe you don't know why your eye keeps gravitating to the closed door in front of you, but maybe He is trying to get your attention. Maybe you've been praying for a confirmation about something, and He is saying it's not for now because right now the door is closed.

We put so many limitations on how God speaks, and as a result we miss so much. Remember, He is God and often chooses the foolish things of man to speak to us. He sent His Son who looked just like us, dressed like us, learned the trade of carpentry, and was a lowly servant, yet He spoke the most powerful message ever spoken in history. It was the message of love and grace that He is still speaking through us, His spiritual conduits.

Don't miss the message because of the package it comes in. The religious made that mistake; they could not see how God could come in that form or package. The fear of being weird and opening your heart to the reality that God may be speaking to you in such simple ways seems to be such a road block for many. If God is truly omnipresent and He lives in you, a born-again believer, then guess what? He is probably trying to speak to you in ways that I believe this section of the book will open up to you.

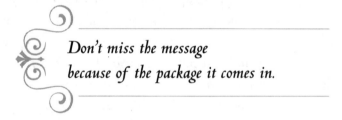

Don't miss the message
because of the package it comes in.

In Jeremiah 1:11 it says, *"Moreover the word of the Lord came to me, saying, 'Jeremiah, what do you see?' And I said, 'I see a branch of an almond tree.'"* Now this could have been a vision or even something he saw in the natural. Either way, God may ask us, "What do you see?" Whether it's something in the natural right in front of us or in a vision, we must pay attention. God can use the natural situation in front of us to relay a prophetic message just like a parable. We think it has to be some spiritual big boom, lightning rod experience with an open vision or an angel walking into the room. It could be as simple as saying, "Shawn, what do you see on the road there?" "Well, I see a black car," or "I see a young man who is on the street alone." God may use something like that to speak to our heart. Let's be open to His communication to us. Let's not be afraid.

> *So he answered, "Do not fear, for those who are with us are more than those who are with them." And Elisha prayed, and said, "Lord, I pray, open his eyes that he may see." Then the Lord opened the eyes of the young man, and he saw. And behold, the mountain was full of horses and chariots of fire all around Elisha* (2 Kings 6:16-17).

At the beginning of this passage, Elisha servant's spiritual eyes were not open. He was reacting in fear based upon what he saw in the natural and was not able to see into the spiritual world surrounding the situation. Often it's not about what you see; it's about what you're not seeing. Don't ask the Lord to close your eyes to the reality in front of you. Ask Him to open your eyes to the unseen reality in front of you. The unseen always trumps what is seen. The servant of Elisha saw in the spirit realm all of the angelic protection God was providing. You need to ask God to open up your spiritual eyes so you can see into the unseen.

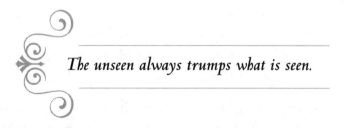

The unseen always trumps what is seen.

There have been seasons in my life when I seem to be more aware of the unseen realm around me. I believe it has to do with the atmosphere cultivated, the people's hunger for the supernatural, and where my focus is at that time. It's similar to finishing a workout for the purpose of building muscle. Although you are tired and sore, your muscles are at their tightest because they have just been stretched. In environments where the supernatural has been really active, often there seems to be a greater awareness and confidence in flowing in the spirit and seeing into the unseen realm. Where visions are the norm, everywhere you go, you have visions and can unlock information in the spirit about people and situations to advance the Kingdom.

I believe we all have an open heaven over us because Jesus tore the veil and broke it open once and for all. Jesus opened the heavens to all mankind once and for all on the cross. It doesn't matter what we do or don't do; our blissful union with Christ is our access point, so we can boldly approach the throne of grace at any moment. It's open to us and for us (see Heb. 4:16). The devil tries to get us to believe that we don't have an open heaven and that we have to work for it, putting us under a yoke of Old Covenant condemnation that declares it's all about our sacrifices, our works, etc. In our new creation state, because of the New Covenant of grace, it's all about His sacrifice and His work that was finished for us. He is the reason we have a continuous open heaven. The principles of the Kingdom such as surrender and sowing and reaping, still apply. But now the difference is that these things are a by-product of our love relationship with Him; we don't have to do these things to appease God or to seek His approval. In the Old Testament the onus was on us; in the New Covenant, the onus is on Him as our substitute. That's why Paul says it's a more glorious covenant.

So even though as born-again believers we have an open heaven, there is still the reality that specific atmospheres and geographical locations seem to have openness and awareness beyond the norm—hence all the various movements of power, revival, renewal, and so on. I believe that these are sovereign moves of God, but they also largely have to do with the believers' position of faith and expectation. In times of great hunger and expectation it seems the visionary realm opens up more clearly. More than a few times I have literally had smoke fill my room. No, it was not a fire or vapor from a hot shower leaking into the hallway and into my room, but while spending time with the Lord literal smoke has filled my room. It's the smoke cloud of His glory like that which was released at the dedication of Solomon's temple when the priests couldn't even stand to minister (see 1 Kings 8:10-11). That's the only way I can describe it. These times with the Lord are and were so amazing and are truly pearls in my life. That type of thing does not happen every day, but when it has, it has been so special.

I was in a mega-church in the United States working in the main office one day, and I needed to ask a question of one of the pastors. As I walked into his office, I noticed that smoke had filled the room. It was so real, in my mind I thought he must be smoking in the office, which would have been ridiculous because there were people all around and the smell would have been obvious. Literally, the whole room was filled with smoke. He had had worship music on and was praying and planning and didn't see it. When I asked him about the smoke and why it was in his office, he looked at me in a funny way. It sounded like I was accusing him of something sketchy. When I realized what I was actually seeing, I felt bad and I said to him, "You don't see that smoke?" and he said, "What do you mean?" We left it at that and I knew then that I had been having an open vision. We don't always have to understand why God allows some to see and others not to see, but we need to celebrate when we do and when others do. This truly honors God.

Visions may not always be a storyboard of events. Sometimes they can be as simple as a snapshot of an image in your mind or superimposed over whatever is in front of you. Whether God gives you a still image in your mind or an open vision as a storyboard of events makes it no more or no less authoritative. A storyboard vision is one that keeps moving, like watching a slide show. Once while I was putting on a conference years ago, I had a very intense visitation from God, and I literally flew back 25 feet onto a couch when one of the guest speakers was prophesying over me. For four and a half hours, the power of God surged through my body like electricity. About half an hour into this experience, I had a snapshot vision of one of the worship leaders. All I saw was her face. I didn't know her very well, but I knew that weekend she had been struggling with some issues. She just looked sad. She was sick and wasn't doing well, and the Lord told me to go prophesy over her. I went and found her and said I believed God wanted to give her a word and asked her if I could pray for her. I put my hand on her head and instantaneously the power of God hit her and she began to weep. As I began to prophesy over her, three angels showed up and I literally could not move for 45 minutes. It felt like I was frozen. I could still prophesy, but I just couldn't move my body. I said, "In three months you are going to have an encounter from God that's going to change and mark your life." Now I had no idea at that moment that three months from that date was her birthday. The Lord did. Three months later to the day on her birthday, she was in a restaurant down south and an angel visited her. It was one of those milestones in her life. This all came through a simple snapshot photo in my mind's eye. It's amazing how the method of communication can seem so simple and yet release such a powerful outcome. Don't doubt just because it may seem like a faint impression.

DREAMS

Biblically, dreams often unveil the destiny, purpose, and plans of God for your life.

Dreams have been a very crucial part of my life and journey with the Lord. I had a dream one night years ago in which a prophet from the U.S. came and looked right at me and said, "Shawn, so I hear you're thinking of having me be your mentor." Then I woke up. The interesting thing is that I had been praying for months about the Lord connecting me with this individual but had no idea how this would happen. Within one month I was invited to his house and sat in his living room while he poured into me and a few others. Never ignore your dreams. Pray into them and position yourself for them to come to pass in your life where you have opportunity.

We see that Joseph in Genesis 37:5 had a dream of his future occupation. The Hebrew word for "dream" means to "bind firmly."[3] When you have a dream from God, it will take root in your heart and become branded upon your spirit. I believe this dream stuck on Joseph like a set of holy handcuffs. The destiny of the dream then determined his circumstances and situations. Even in the midst of exile and being sold into slavery, he was bound to that dream firmly. Even though he felt discouraged, frustrated, and probably at times like it was never going to happen. Something took hold in his heart that enabled him to be obedient throughout all the testing, so the dream could actually manifest itself in his life.

> *Until the time came to fulfill his dreams, the Lord tested Joseph's character* (Psalm 105:19 NLT).

Whenever God gives you a promise through a prophetic word, in His wisdom He shapes your life circumstance in relation to that word. This is designed to shape your character and prepare you for what He has for you. Let your season mentor you into the person He's called you to be so that you will be able to handle the promise given to you.

God loves to meet the need, but He also loves the process between believing for the need to be met and it actually happening.

Our faith muscle and expectation of what God can and wants to do in and through us keep on growing. What I can believe for now is in accordance with my revelation of God's nature, season, level of maturity, and experience. We grow into the grace over our lives. We grow into all that God has already given to us through time and faith. So it's not an issue of not having it, but of readiness and maturity. God bestows on us what we can handle according to the season we are in.

> *God bestows on us what we can handle according to the season we are in.*

Years ago when I first started out in ministry, I moved to Alaska and had to fly to Seattle first. I had felt the Lord was asking me to go to Israel and Africa but really had no money. I had had a few weeks to really pray about this but it seemed like there was no provision for the trip. I remember the pastor of the church I was a part of let me speak in the fireside prayer room of the church that night for anyone who wanted to hear what the Lord was doing in and through my life in that season. That morning someone had blessed me with $200 for my trip to Israel and Africa. Obviously this was not enough, as I needed over $4,000 Canadian. Although it was something, and I was thankful. The Lord said to me to give that $200 into the offering that morning. So I did, obviously with the thought, *But God, isn't this Your provision for me?* God loves to test the heart. It's not about finances but about wisdom and faith. This set something into motion, and that night after the meeting, someone walked up to me and gave me another $200. Then the following morning another few hundred dollars appeared in my mailbox. Then that night—the night before I had to leave—I had a dream that was quite allegorical in nature. By giving the details of the dream, perhaps you will see patterns to look for in your own dream life.

In my dream, I saw two floating bottles of the body wash Truth by Calvin Klein, which was what I used at the time. Often God will use symbols that occupy your current life and situation to speak to you, for the purpose of clarity and understanding. I remember thinking, *That's more than enough truth than I really need.* Jesus is the truth (see John 14:6) and in Him there is *always more than enough.* His name is El Shaddai, the God who is all sufficient and full of abundant blessing. Sometimes the Body of Christ needs a good "wash with the truth" that Jesus is the God of more than enough and that He is not *just* Jehovah Jireh the provider but also El Shaddai. Soon after, in my dream, I was handed a check for $3,000 U.S. for my trip to Israel and Africa. With the other money I had from a few days before, it was equivalent to what I needed. When I woke up from this dream, I knew it had tremendous significance and that something was going to happen. As I was getting ready to leave my house to drive to the airport, I got a phone call from a couple. They said they wanted to see me before I flew out to Seattle. I went over and they sat me down and said, "Shawn, God woke us up last night and said to us, 'Give Shawn your entire savings account.'" I was floored. I'd had a dream that night, and at the same time to confirm it, God had woken them up to speak to them. They wrote me a check for $4,000 Canadian, which was close to $3,000 U.S. at that time, plus a Ziploc® bag full of American spending money. It was "more than enough," just as in my dream. I was amazed at the faithfulness of God.

TRANCES

God also speaks in what the Bible calls trances. One of the most well-known references to this is found in Acts 10:9-16, describing Peter on the housetop where God commissioned him to preach the gospel to the Gentile community.

> *The next day, as they went on their journey and drew near the city, Peter went up on the housetop to pray, about the sixth hour. Then he became very hungry and wanted to eat; but while they made ready,* **he fell into a trance and saw heaven opened** *and an object like a great sheet bound at the four corners, descending to him and let down to the earth. In it were all kinds of four-footed animals of the earth, wild beasts, creeping things, and birds of the air.* **And a voice came to him, "Rise, Peter; kill and eat."** *But Peter said, "Not so, Lord! For I have never eaten anything common or unclean."* **And a voice spoke to him the second time, "What God has cleansed you must not call common."** *This was done three times. And the object was taken up into heaven again* (Acts 10:9-16).

A trance is the state you fall into to have an experience or a vision. It's like going into a dreamlike or daydreaming state, but you are awake. The English transliteration of the Greek word for "trance" is *ecstasy*, the "displacing [of] the individual's ordinary state of mind with an elevated, God-given state for the purpose of instructing him."[4] Peter went into this state and then had the vision, and in the vision a voice spoke to him.

Paul had a revelation in the midst of a trance while praying in the temple, and God told to him to get out of Jerusalem (see Acts 22:17-21).

In our traveling ministry, God has often taken me into a trance to reveal words of knowledge about individuals who will be in the meetings. Many times He has revealed names, numbers, and so on that bring faith for the purpose of healings and miracles. Once I was in a meeting in Northern Quebec, in a small native community where there were only a few white people. In the afternoon between the meetings I was planning to sleep for a few hours. I began to pray and then fell into a trance. In the trance, I saw a white man, balding on top, with grayish facial hair and a droopy face, plus many other details. God spoke to me during the vision and said, "He has had a stomach disorder since 1986." When I came out of this trance state, I thought to myself, *God, there are only a few white people so far that have been in these meetings, and I know what they all look like.* I recorded the details of this experience in my mind, knowing it was the Lord speaking to me. When I got to the meeting, there was no one who fit that description, and only a few white men at that. During worship, a few walked in and one sat behind me who looked identical to what I had seen in the trance. While I was ministering to the people, I called this man up. He had come from a neighboring town quite far away. I began to explain that I believed God had shown him to me in a vision, and he was blown away because he in fact had had a stomach disorder since 1986. He began to weep as God began to touch his stomach with His healing power. It was a powerful experience for him.

One other time I was traveling and had a few connecting flights to catch. While on the first flight, I fell into a trance as I was praying. I saw myself in the next airport, getting onto another plane. I remember noticing that something very significant was going to happen. During this experience, God said to me, "Prepare yourself in prayer for what is about to come." On the next plane, I sat beside a middle-aged man and knew that something was going to happen to him. God began to speak to me about his life and I began to share it with him. The power of God hit him and he began to cry and said to me, "I want to know this Jesus Christ." When I shared with him that God had shown me on the other flight what was going to happen, he was powerfully impacted and had his first encounter with Jesus Christ.

STILL SMALL VOICE

First Kings 19:11-13 says that it wasn't in the wind or quake or fire but in a still small voice that the Lord spoke to Elijah. Sometimes God speaks in a delicate whisper (still small voice). Sometimes this method can have the most powerful outcome even though it may seem very faint. Many think that when God speaks in the still small voice the outcome will be less powerful than if God were to send an angel. When God speaks, however, it is always powerful no matter the method He chooses to use to communicate to us.

> *When God speaks, it is always powerful no matter the method He chooses to use to communicate to us.*

VISITATIONS OF GOD

There are times where we can honestly say, "Wow, that was a visit from God." I know that as born-again believers we have a habitation of God on the inside. God is in us and with us everywhere we go. But there are special times when there is an increased awareness of His presence and power, when He makes Himself known to us in a more powerful, visible way. As a nonbelieving murderer of Christians, Saul who then became Paul had a visitation from God (see Acts 9:3) on the road to Damascus that transformed his life. This encounter changed his life forever and was the beginning of a new focus and mandate in his life. In Genesis 18:1-15, three angels visited Abraham and left him and his wife, Sarah, with the promise of a son. Often when we have powerful encounters like this, the Lord leaves something life-altering with us. God communicates in and through wild encounters with Him. Bring it on, God!

THE AUDIBLE AND INNER AUDIBLE VOICE OF GOD

In the Old Testament God often spoke in an audible voice. When God speaks with an inner audible voice, everything vibrates and shakes on the inside of you. This is not like His still small voice or other ways of communication. One night not too long ago after a meeting, I was driving near where I live at 1:30 in the morning and saw three guys walking on the street. They had come out of the bar and were obviously drunk or on drugs. God spoke to me in what felt like a scream inside me, saying, "Stop!" then told me to go back to them. I did a U-turn and pulled to the side of the road. When I got out of the car I began to chase after them, which must have looked pretty funny, thinking about it afterward. When I got to them, God began to give me some insight into one guy's life and, as a result, one of the others standing beside him was touched by the power of Jesus. The power of God came all over one of them, showing him that Jesus was the real deal. It was a powerful experience. Another time as I was driving to visit someone in jail, I heard very loud in my spirit, "You're not going to visit (the person's name), but you're going to visit Me." The scripture immediately came to mind of Matthew 25:336, which says, *"...I was in prison and you came to Me."* In verse 40, Jesus explains what He meant, saying, *"Assuredly, I say to you, inasmuch as you did it to one of the least of these My brethren, you did it to Me."* If Jesus were on this earth in the flesh, we would find Him in the dark, oppressed areas of society releasing His light and love. When we go where He would go, we touch the very heart of Jesus. In both these cases, God spoke to me with an inner audible voice.

HOLY GHOST REMINDERS

One of the most amazing ways that God speaks to us is by bringing things back to our memory. We know Holy Spirit's job is to bring back to remembrance truths of who Jesus is (see John 14:26), but I believe He also brings back testimonies and reminders of words that we have given to others to speak to us in our present situation.

There will be times when you may be ministering to someone, and God will bring you back to a similar situation in the past. Holy Spirit may say, "Remember that word you had way back? I want you to give a similar word to the person in front of you right now." Or you may be struggling with a situation and have trouble believing in God's faithfulness, so Holy Spirit will remind you of past situations where He showed Himself faithful to you to bring you back into faith.

FEELINGS, EMOTIONS, OR IMPRESSIONS

This is often the way that people, both prophets and the like, hear from the Lord. It can be as simple as a feeling, emotion, or an impression upon the heart. When I lived in Minnesota, I lived in the basement of a family's house. The mother of the household really had a special grace for interpreting dreams. I had a dream one night that I was walking with Jesus down a hallway, and as I was walking I can remember the most amazing feeling of love, a love that was far out of my earthly grid and understanding. As we continued to walk down the hallway, He let me go. The moment this happened, this intense overwhelming emotion came over me in the dream and I began to weep uncontrollably. The next day, I went to the woman of the house and told her the dream and asked her what she felt. As she began to open her mouth, it was like this supernatural wind came into the room right into her body. All of sudden she began to weep. She then began to interpret the dream as Holy Spirit gave her what seemed to be the exact same emotion that I had experienced in the dream. Holy Spirit let her feel exactly what I felt in the dream so she could interpret it for me. It was such a wild experience. In this case, His voice and the interpretation of the dream for me manifested in and through her feelings and emotions.

Often when ministering at a church or on the street, I have an impression or a thought cross my mind like the name of a city, a name, a number, or some other random information. More times than not, it's Holy Spirit speaking to me. I was in Ireland a few years ago, and as I looked over at these two men Holy Spirit was highlighting to me, the state of South Carolina kept crossing my mind over and over. I found out after I ministered to them that they were from South Carolina and were missionaries to Ireland. Holy Spirit speaks in this way and yet often people will miss it. I was glad I hadn't missed this opportunity because of how small the impression had been.

DISCERNING SMELLS

Psalm 45:8 says, *"All Your garments are scented with myrrh and aloes and cassia, out of the ivory palaces, by which they have made You glad."* Exodus 30:23-25 speaks of similar ingredients used in the holy anointing oil that was for the tabernacle of meeting, as well as for anointing Aaron and his sons as priests. Jesus is the anointed one and when His fragrance comes into a room, it is recognizable. Calvin Klein has nothing on the anointed one, Jesus Christ. There are smells in Heaven that would be recognizable and others that we have never smelled before. God can and does sometimes allow His people to smell for the purpose of discernment and insight into what He is doing. The devil's kingdom is also associated with specific smells, such as sulfur, as noted in Revelation 9:18 and 19:20. So, when a demon is present, it can often be discerned through the sense of smell.

SPONTANEOUS GOD THOUGHTS

This is one of the most common ways God speaks. You could be praying, driving, or jogging your morning jog, and all of a sudden, you'll think of someone you know. Then maybe you see that person as you are jogging, and you're like, "Oh my, what a coincidence." *It's not a coincidence!* There are no coincidences in Kingdom life, only appointments from God. He has ordered your steps and knows everything. When this happens, ask God what He wants to do, acknowledging that this is no coincidence. Maybe you're driving to the grocery store and you think of someone you haven't thought of for years, and then you see him or her at the grocery store. Many reading this can attest to this experience, believing it was just a coincidence. I encourage you to consider that God may be speaking to you and to ask Him what He wants to say. These may seem like simple coincidences, but perhaps you've just been missing recognizing His voice the whole time.

RECOGNIZING THE FAMILIAR

You're about to be blown away now. Are you ready? Recognizing someone as familiar is one of the most interesting ways God has spoken to me, and 80 percent of the people I talk to have had this happen to them as well. There have been times when I've looked at someone and I know I do not know that person, but something about him or her is very familiar. The person may remind me of someone I know or know of and may even have the same name. The person he or she reminds me of may be an amazing artist or musician, a businessperson, or a very studious individual. Often God is showing me that this person has a similar call and gift, or similar traits and character to the one I am reminded of. God may do this to let you know that He wants to do something similar in that individual's life. If God shows you something in this way, ask Him what He wants to do. I have personally seen powerful encounters come of this method of communication.

DARK SAYINGS OR RIDDLES

A dark saying is simply a riddle. Yes, God did and still does speak in riddles. You may say, "You're kidding, right?" We read about it in

Numbers 12:8, speaking of Moses: *"I speak with him face to face, even plainly, and not in dark sayings; and he sees the form of the Lord...."* The literal translation of a dark saying is a riddle, which is defined as a "puzzle, hence, a trick, conundrum, sententious maxim...hard question, proverb."[5]

> *Give ear, O my people, to my law; incline your ears to the words of my mouth. I will open my mouth in a parable; I will utter dark sayings of old* (Psalm 78:1-2).

> *For now we see in a mirror, dimly* [in a riddle], *but then face to face. Now I know in part, but then I shall know just as I also am known. And now abide faith, hope, love, these three; but the greatest of these is love* (I Corinthians 13:12-13).

A dark saying (or riddle)—which is what this scripture of First Corinthians 13 is—in many ways is the Old Testament equivalent to a parable. It is "dim" in appearance at first glance, yet full of treasure and wisdom as it's sought out and unpacked. God spoke to the prophets this way in the Old Testament. In the New Testament, Jesus spoke the equivalent in parable form (dimly). A parable in many ways is enigmatic, full of hidden truth for those who are willing to seek it out.

I woke up one morning to a loud, audible voice of God speaking to me, saying, the "bitter taste of the sweet almond will be the sound of your deliverance." It was so profound that I actually thought I was hearing a Proverb. So I searched for it in the Scriptures and found nothing. I really prayed and thought about this for weeks. Then God started to bring clarity and show me the connection between the almond and leadership in Scripture, such as when Aaron's rod budded almond blossoms and produced almonds (see Num. 17:8). There is a bitter and a sweet side to leadership as there are always challenges to face. According to tradition, the rod had sweet almonds on one side and bitter almonds on the other.[6] God began to unpack what this riddle meant for my life, and is still revealing it to this very day. It was that profound.

NUMBERS AND SYMBOLS THAT ARE REPEATED

If you were to study numerology in the Bible, you would realize very quickly that numbers have much prophetic significance and meaning, as do colors, certain objects, and animals. You will find that studying their meaning will provide context for scripture, clarify your dream life, and make His communication to you clearer. For instance, if you see repeated numbers like 333, 111, 222, 1111 many times a day, then begin to ask Holy Spirit for answers. You are better off to ask than to ignore. Don't worry about being over-spiritual. I don't know about you, but I would rather be over-spiritual than under-spiritual. You have more of a chance of succeeding on the former than you do on the latter.

> *I don't know about you, but I would rather be over-spiritual than under-spiritual.*

The Lord has always been specific with me on important events that would take place at certain ages of my life. When I was 21, words began to come to me about the importance of my 22nd year. Then when I turned 22, it was like the Lord decided to remind me every day of the importance of that year by prompting me to see 11:11, which when added together equals 22, several times a day for that entire year. I saw it on license plates and noticed it everywhere I went. I could not ignore it. God was clearly trying to grab my attention. At 22, I met my wife, Michelle, and was launched into full-time ministry through an incredible angelic encounter in North Carolina. It was a very significant year. Remember that everything in our life happens for a reason. God cares about every little detail of our life. He is trying to communicate with us every day, and many of us don't even realize it.

> *The Lord directs the steps of the godly, He delights in every detail of their lives* (Psalm 37:23 NLT).

God loves each of His children so much that He may be speaking, or will speak, to each of us in an entirely unique way. He knows us so intimately that He will tailor His communication to our specific level of spiritual maturity, our circumstances, and our willingness to accept His word no matter what the package. The choice is ours to lean into Holy Spirit and open our senses to understanding the language of His Spirit.

ENDNOTES

1. Hayford, ed., *Spirit-Filled Life Bible*, commentary for Mark 4:2.

2. Albert Barnes, *Notes on the Bible* (1834, text courtesy of Internet Sacred Texts Archive), Online Parallel Bible, accessed January 18, 2012, http://bible.cc/daniel/7-15.htm.

3. Hayford, ed., *Spirit-Filled Life Bible*, "Kingdom Dynamics" commentary for Genesis 37:5.

4. Ibid., commentary on Acts 10:9-10.

5. Numbers 12:8, lexicon, Online Bible, accessed March 5, 2012, http://scripturetext.com/numbers/12-8.htm.

6. Wikipedia, s.v., "almond," last updated March 1, 2012, http://en.wikipedia.org/wiki/Almond.

CHAPTER 8

DETECTING COUNTERFEITS

And no wonder! For Satan himself transforms himself into an angel of light. (2 Corinthians 11:14)

ONE of the greatest hurdles to get over when operating in the supernatural is the fear of deception. Because of the abuse, negative experiences, or latest "Christian Hollywood" gossip about a man or woman of God falling, people are bound by the fear of being deceived. Destiny is held in the balance when people operate this way. *What if I make a mistake? What if someone I look up to deceives me?* There are endless "what if" scenarios, but when you realize that ultimately you are not in control, you can liberate yourself by simply trusting in Holy Spirit's ability to keep you from deception. Proverbs gives us a sure promise of straight and directed paths when we trust in and acknowledge God in every situation and season of life.

Trust in the Lord with all your heart, and lean not on your own understanding; in all your ways acknowledge Him, and He shall direct your paths (Proverbs 3:5-6).

Some people put more faith in the enemy's power and ability to deceive them than in Holy Spirit's ability to protect them from deception. We never win with fear or unbelief. I would rather fail because of faith and stepping out to trust the Lord than to never step out at all because of fear and unbelief. In God's eyes, faith always wins. It pleases Him (see Heb. 11:6). By not trusting in God in every area, we give place for faith to be invested in the enemy's abilities and power to take us out. Faith and trust in Jesus accesses the grace that enables us to overcome these hurdles in our spiritual life. Remember, faith is a gift of grace that enables us to live the abundant life that Jesus promised we would have.

Faith is a gift of grace that enables us to live the abundant life that Jesus promised we would have.

We are called to a lifestyle of faith, not just to have faith in a few "easy" areas of our lives. Believing we will get to Heaven is not hard for most, but to believe God in finances, health, families, and the like seems to be hard for many. Paul encouraged the church at Thessalonica to close the gaps of their faith. First Thessalonians 3:9-10 in the New Living Translation says:

*How we thank God for you! Because of you we have great joy as we enter God's presence. Night and day we pray earnestly for you, asking God to let us see you again **to fill the gaps in your faith**.*

God wants faith to be evident in and permeate every area of our lives. The grace gift of faith in Christ's finished work gives us access to see His promises manifest in our lives. Your faith will create room for what He has already promised. If you don't believe that God wants to heal you as a believer, outside of God's sovereignty you won't access healing. What you believe about Christ determines what you empower and allow access into your life.

The devil loves when we give him credit and believe more in his power to deceive us and mess us up, than in God's power to keep us safe. This is why many people never step into a supernatural lifestyle. They're too afraid of being wrong and misrepresenting God. God is big enough to handle our mistakes! I'm not saying that we should say whatever comes to us, thinking that God will clean up all of our messes. What I am saying is, don't let the fear of failure stop you from stepping out in the supernatural and prophetic, representing the Kingdom life on earth that you are called to represent.

LEARNING FROM MISTAKES

Most people don't have a problem with this "mistakes are a part of life" mindset in their secular workplace. People develop in a workplace by solving problems and learning from mistakes. If we can make a few mistakes on a new job and know that our manager won't fire us, then why can't we have the same attitude with God and the Kingdom? God is even more loving, more gracious, and more caring than any boss. But sometimes we act like we don't believe that. We need to remember that faith pleases the Father even if sometimes we make mistakes (see Heb. 11:6).

God is not up in the sky waiting for our name to show up on the naughty list so He can beat us with His shepherd's rod and make sure we learn our lesson. He is interested in training us just as any good parent would train his or her child. Hebrews 12:6 says, *"For whom the Lord loves He chastens, and scourges every son whom He receives."* The word *chasten* here means child training and giving instruction. Because God loves us, He will use seasons in our lives to train us to become the people we are destined to be. The truth is that every one of us has made mistakes, but the key is to learn from the mistakes and move on to maturity. We shouldn't be inviting and welcoming mistakes; instead, we know they are part of the growth and maturing process. Instead of thinking, *What if I step out and prophesy. . .and I'm wrong?* We should ask ourselves, *Is my heart right? Am I learning and desiring to step out?*

NEW COVENANT WINE TESTER

Many leaders and people within the Body of Christ aggressively attack what some call the prophetic or charismatic movement. They say if someone's prophecy is wrong, then he or she is a false prophet. If this were true, then this principle would have to apply across the board within every respected office calling (see Eph. 4:11). This would then mean that if a teacher had a revelation of Christ that he or she did not know before and was teaching the opposite at one point, then that person could have been considered a false teacher. Or if a local pastor gave wrong advice to a couple in the church or said something he or she shouldn't have said while upset, he or she could be considered a false pastor. And this same principle would apply to the apostle and evangelist as well. This is not the benchmark for what the New Testament revelation of prophets or fivefold ministry is today. It is no longer just about the accuracy of a word. This is why the office of the prophet seems to get lambasted the most in the Body of Christ.

When we operate in the supernatural, there must be room to grow. We can't and shouldn't expect perfection and flawlessness. This is totally unreasonable and not a reflection of the New Covenant. (I liken this attitude to a natural father who never stepped up to his responsibilities to advise or discipline his children for fear of making a wrong judgment call or giving wrong advice. We can't live in fear.)

You may be thinking, *Well, what about the Old Testament when it talks about the test of a true prophet of the Lord?* Deuteronomy 18 speaks of the word coming to pass or not as the test of whether a prophet is from the Lord or not.

> *"But the prophet who presumes to speak a word in My name, which I have not commanded him to speak, or who speaks in the name of other gods, that prophet shall die." And if you say in your heart, "How shall we know the word which the Lord has not spoken?"—* **when a prophet speaks in the name of the Lord, if the thing does not happen or come to pass, that is the thing which the Lord has not spoken;** *the prophet has spoken it presumptuously; you shall not be afraid of him* (Deuteronomy 18:20-22).

To bring clarity on this subject, remember that the Spirit of the Lord was not accessible to the average individual before Christ came on the scene. The priests, prophets, judges, kings, and queens had the Spirit of the Lord on them to complete whatever specific task they were assigned. There were a select few who had the authority to lead with anointing for a specific task. The Spirit of the Lord could rest on an individual and lift off an individual for various reasons and seasons. These mediators, specifically the prophets in this time, were in many ways bridges to the Father Himself.

In Exodus 7:1, the New Living Translation says, *"Then the Lord said to Moses, 'Pay close attention to this. I will make you seem like God to Pharaoh, and your brother, Aaron, will be your prophet.'"* Moses was the mediator between God and Pharaoh as well as between Israel and God. Many during that time would seek out prophets for guidance, or a seer for insight and a word from the Lord because the common man or woman did not have access to hear from Heaven outside of God sovereignly visiting him or her.

The responsibility of leadership in the Old Testament was intense. There were only a few who had the Spirit of the Lord on them and the anointing to be God's representatives, so there was no room for error when declaring the word of the Lord. These individuals were the trusted spiritual sources and counsel for spiritual matters, so the test of true and false prophets was whether the word came to pass.

In the New Covenant, Jesus brought in a whole new way to test the purity of the wine that would come forth. Because of Christ's sacrifice on the cross, He tore the veil between all mankind and the Father. Through the blood of Jesus Christ, we have been given free access to the Father and the door is wide open for those who choose to walk through it. We now all have access to a relationship with God, to hear and recognize His voice and represent Him and His finished work on the cross for the reconciliation of humankind.

> *The door of free access to the Father is wide open for those who choose to walk through it.*

We are not all prophets, but we all have a prophetic nature because we have been born again of the seed of Heaven. We are all kings and priests according to Revelation 5:10. We have perfect union with Jesus as born-again believers and are constantly seeing an unveiling of Christ day after day. This revelation gives us the assurance that we have the ability to discern and filter out things that do not glorify Him. We are no longer *just* to assess whether or not someone is a false or true prophet by his or her prophetic word; we also are to test the spirit behind the word and individual. First John 4:1 speaks of a new way of testing and judging—by the spirit of the word and individual.

> *Beloved, do not believe every spirit, but **test the spirits,** whether they are of God; because many false prophets have gone out into the world* (I John 4:1).

We are still called to weigh every word and judge every word. Paul encourages the church at Corinth to judge prophetic words (see I Cor. 14:29), and in First Thessalonians 5:19-21 he says, *"Do not quench the Spirit. Do not despise prophecies. Test all things; hold fast what is good."* The focus in the New Covenant is to test the spirit behind the individual and the word, not the word only.

So in the Old Testament, we are called to test the word; in the New, we are called to test the spirit behind the word. Just as the Old Covenant was all about the law, the New Covenant is all about the Spirit of life. Faith accesses righteousness, not obedience to the letter of the

219

law. Obedience is now a result of right standing and right believing in the good news of the gospel of love and grace. So we are not to apply an Old Testament method of testing a prophet to today's New Testament culture.

The Body of Christ would be in trouble if our method of discernment was built on the accuracy of someone's word. Many in the Body of Christ would be following psychics, mediums, and occult leaders. For this very reason, many have left the faith and joined cults and followed leaders who have been exposed as purporting deceptive fallacies. Unfortunately, many of these leaders have prophesied accurate time lines and words, so we cannot rely on those results to discern whether they are of God or not.

We must learn to test the spirit of an individual. *Is Jesus being honored, glorified, and lifted up? Are people encountering the love of Jesus and being transformed?* These are good questions to ask yourself when assessing any particular word. *Who is the focus? Jesus or the individual?*

Even if the one prophesying clearly has a pride problem and seems to be boasting about himself, if Jesus is being made known as Lord and the one way, the truth, and the life, then chances are he is not a false prophet; he may just may have some Daddy issues. Having perfect doctrine in every area of spiritual matters does not determine whether someone is good or bad. Jesus is perfect doctrine; He is the filter for every pure wine test. Just be sure the main thing stays the main thing—Jesus and Him crucified and resurrected for our new life, for the forgiveness of our sin, giving us the gift of righteousness and right standing with Him.

Acts 16:16-19 recounts a story of a slave girl, a fortune-teller who had a spirit of divination, who followed Paul and Silas as they were on their way to prayer. For many days, she followed the two men and cried out, saying, *"These men are the servants of the Most High God, who proclaim to us the way of salvation."*

She clearly was discerning right with accurate revelation even though she was not living that reality herself. In fact, she was living an opposing lifestyle to what she was proclaiming as truth. She was spiritually entrenched in herself and her divination. Paul eventually became greatly annoyed and agitated in his spirit, and he rebuked the spirit and cast out the demon from her. So here's an example where the fortune-teller was proclaiming accurate information. She could discern it, even though she was not experiencing it. Imagine if because of her accuracy people credited her as one sent from God Himself. She could have had quite a following and led the latest cult.

In an era where there is so much spiritual mixture and hybrid religions and practices, we must not fall into the trap of just looking at the words themselves. Although that is good, we must also test the spirit behind the words, and that's exactly what Paul discerned. I can't tell you how many times in our meetings we have had people come who say all the right things and sound like Spirit-filled believers, yet I can discern a mocking spirit over them that's fueling all they say. Think about it for a moment. Imagine all the local fortune-tellers and psychics in your community proclaiming that your church had the message of truth and life. Even though that could be and should be true of our churches, we can't let the truth of someone's word be the scale to weigh someone's credibility as a messenger from God. We cannot rely on an Old Testament model; we must rely on the Spirit's discernment in us—just like Paul did.

We must get over the fear of being deceived and making mistakes. We must know the Word of God, and we must test the spirit. A solid supernatural life will follow when faith is present and fear is excommunicated. Focusing on the truth of Jesus Christ will be our greatest asset in detecting counterfeits and positioning our lives for an everyday supernatural life experience.

CHAPTER 9

OUR INTIMATE UNION
WITH CHRIST

*I have been crucified with Christ; it is no longer I who live, but
Christ lives in me; and the life which I now live in the flesh I live
by faith in the Son of God, who loved me and gave Himself for
me.* (Galatians 2:20)

YOU are now one with Christ if you have received the forgiveness that was released for your sin through Christ's death on the
cross. You are a two-in-one combination now—Christ in you! This
revelation initiates such desire to understand what the experience in
and through your union with Christ really looks like. Principally you
cannot get any closer to Christ than you are right now because you are
united as one. From day to day you come into a greater experience of
that oneness and so mature in that relationship. It is a life of unfolding

and discovery, which is what makes our relationship with Him so fun and exciting. However, the process of discovery to this reality begins with desire. It has been my prayer since the beginning that leaders in the Body of Christ would model the kind of hunger and supernatural experiential intimacy described in Exodus 33:11. The Scripture promises that there is a greater glory in the New Covenant compared to the glory that was on Moses' life. How much further can we go? We have been united permanently with Jesus, buried with Him and raised to new life, manifested as a new creation on the inside. We have 24-hour, on-tap access to the Lord. We are holy tabernacles of the glory. No longer do we have to go into a physical tent to meet with the Lord because we are that tent for His presence and glory. Moses went in and out, but the Scriptures say in Exodus 33:11 that Joshua did not depart from that place. And he ended up leading the children of Israel into the Promised Land. As born-again believers we live there always, never departing or able to be separated from that place of His presence and glory.

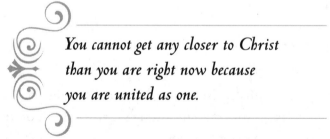

You cannot get any closer to Christ than you are right now because you are united as one.

In the Old Covenant, the cloud of glory moved among the people and guided them. Before the New Covenant, the cloud of glory came in the form of flesh—Jesus Christ—and moved among them. In the New Covenant, after Jesus' death, burial, and resurrection, the cloud of glory is made manifest through the Body of Christ—the believers—moving among all humanity.

Joshua, who was Moses' protégé and successor, learned from the best. He saw the consistency of his leader and mentor Moses when it came to spending time with the Lord to build a trusting relationship and to receive the counsel and direction needed to lead Israel out of Egypt and into the Promised Land effectively. Joshua not only caught on to this, but he also received an incredible hunger and desire to spend quality time with the Lord.

Moses went to the tent of meeting and visited with God face to face as a man speaks to a friend. God gave Moses supernatural counsel for leadership. Joshua saw this and became hungry for the presence of God. Joshua would stay hours after Moses left the tent of meeting with God. He would stay and linger in the presence of God.

We need the hunger that Joshua had, but we can't make that happen by ourselves; it first starts with a revelation of Jesus Christ and His love and grace. What we can do is feed on the person of Christ, which empowers and strengthens our spirit. If we are always feeding ourselves garbage, we will feel like garbage. This is why quality time with the Lord is so crucial. But it must come from a right perspective of our intimate union with Jesus Christ (see 1 Cor. 6:17). So if you spend all your time watching movies, playing video games, and just vegging out, then chances are you won't feel alive in your spirit. If that's all you are doing every day, chances are you have never really encountered the love and goodness of God or have forgotten what He is like.

A revelation of who Jesus Christ is and what He has done for us changes our situational reality. It produces life. He wants to be our priority. In the natural, the more we eat, the more our stomach stretches— and usually, over time, we gain more capacity for food, which means we get hungrier and eat more. As you reduce the amount you eat, eventually you aren't as hungry as you were before. He wants to be the object of your affections and satisfy you at the deepest place.

> *I shall be fully satisfied, when I awake [to find myself] behold-*
> *ing Your form [and having sweet communion with You]* (Psalm
> 17:15b AMP).

Let this be your heart's desire.

INTIMACY WITH CHRIST
AND WITH OTHERS

We were not destined to be alone. We need people and people need us. We were designed for relationships. The first relationship priority is with God, then with other people. There is actually part of your life that not even God was destined to fill. Genesis 2:18 says, *"And the Lord God said, 'It is not good that man should be alone; I will make him a helper comparable to him.'"* In the midst of perfection before the fall of man and sin entered the world, God, the Creator of the universe and of humankind, made the statement that it was not good for man to be alone. God saw a need. It wasn't that God made a mistake when making Adam; He created Adam with the need for a companion. It doesn't matter if you are called to singleness or marriage, we all need people in our lives. Jesus highlighted it, the Acts church modeled it, and the Hebrews writer declared it:

> *Not forsaking the assembling of ourselves together, as is the manner*
> *of some, but exhorting one another, and so much the more as you see*
> *the Day approaching* (Hebrews 10:25).

To be fully satisfied in Him is to receive all the benefits of how He created us to be with Him and others. He created us for fellowship. We don't go to church Sunday mornings to be fed. Our feeding is on the finished work of Jesus day by day, walking in intimate union with Him. The primary purpose of our Sunday gathering with other believers is to worship together in unity, encourage one another, and be in fellowship. People say to me, "I'm leaving my church because I don't get fed there." That is a selfish perspective. The primary purpose of fellowship is not about what you can get out of it, but what you can give. The reality? It works both ways. When we give, we receive. Some don't give, and then feel like they don't receive. Don't get me wrong; being fed spiritually in church on a Sunday morning should be happening for sure, but that can't be our primary purpose in showing up. Advancing, life-giving church communities have a culture of a day-to-day, Spirit-led life. Struggling, dry, and dull church communities have a culture of pew warmers who think they have a ticket to Heaven if they attend and are "good, faithful church people."

The greater purpose of a Sunday morning church service—or whenever your main gathering time is—should be celebration. We need to come to church ready to celebrate all that God is, entering His courts with praise and thanksgiving (see Ps. 100:4).

The best avenue for equipping and teaching is in meetings during the week or in schools designed to hone in on certain aspects of Kingdom life. Let hunger build during the week by focusing on the beauty of Jesus every day, so when you enter His house Sunday morning you come to give—not just receive. People who come Sunday morning and generally feel dead spiritually are those who don't eat during the week. They don't feel like giving in worship or even engaging people in conversation. When we don't eat of His goodness day to day and feast on the revelation of the finished work of the cross, it's easy to become bored, dull, and spiritually unaware. Pastors sometimes feel like they are taking out their spoons Sunday morning to jam the food down the people's throats. There are many people sitting in pews each Sunday morning thinking, *Wake me up, feed me, give to me.* They are often the ones who say, "I don't get anything from church." If you're eating of God's Word and Spirit, you're going to have a different response, a different reaction, when you come to church. You won't want to leave. No longer will the local chicken house down the road keep you checking your watch. My encouragement to you is to find time to eat of Him every day. Find quality time with the Lord like you do for your spouse, best friend, or child. Get into the Word, and have some conversations with Big G.

FACE TO FACE WITH GOD

Moses was a revolutionary, a prophetic leader, and a voice to the Israelites. He had a supernatural intimacy with God at a level that not many had. He knew and understood the concept of relationship and the importance of God's presence. Standing in the counsel of God and spending time with Him gave Moses the right and ability to speak on behalf of God, and he became one of the most humble leaders and prophetic voices of his time.

The prophetic has to come out of intimacy with God. Moses understood this truth. He probably thought to himself, *If I don't stand in the counsel of God, face to face with God, I cannot be the effective leader that I'm called to be for this nation.* Don't condemn yourself if you only pray five minutes a day—don't think you are doomed. Or maybe you are thinking, *I'm never going to get past ten minutes.* Everyone is in a process—let the Lord lead you.

Our relationship with the Lord is mirrored by the union and relationship we have with our spouses (see Eph. 5:22-33). God destined it that way for lots of reasons. It's easier for us to establish a relational, spiritual model from an earthly one. The same way we build strong healthy relationships with our spouses, we can build a strong healthy relationship with the Lord—by investing time with Him because we understand His investment in us. Yes, there are some dynamically different components to our relationship with the Lord, but at the very least let's use the time-invested component. We need focused time with Him.

Imagine spending only five minutes a day with your spouse. After ten years, you probably wouldn't have much depth to your relationship. Yes, you will have knowledge and may even know what he or she likes, but the deep things are found in the pursuit and time invested in your spouse. If you go on vacation for a week and spend 24 hours a day focused on your spouse, you will create a level of intimacy that could never be experienced by spending five minutes a day for an entire year. After that week together, the moment you're apart, you will most likely miss him or her. Time invested produces fruit. What is time when you're in love? Remember when you first met your spouse and hours would go by, spent just by talking? It felt like minutes. It's not a burden when you're in love.

The more time we invest, the more we will access because we will have an energized faith—and, I believe, the more God will reveal to us. Now hear me: it's not a striving thing where God's not going to speak to you if you don't spend more than ten minutes a day with Him. God will use anything we give Him, but like stewardship, the more we use, the more it multiplies and advances in and through our lives. Those who spend little to no time with the Lord, when hearing this, either get furiously upset and offended or stirred up and encouraged. Choose to be challenged in your relationship with Him, not offended. God *"is a rewarder of those who diligently seek Him"* (Heb. 11:6). Stare at the beauty of His face and let Him love you the way He wants to.

OBEDIENCE

John 14:15 says, *"If you love Me, keep My commandments."* This was a statement made by Jesus before He died and paid the price for all humankind to live in freedom. In the Old Covenant, emphasis was placed on what we did and didn't do, on our works. In the New Covenant, the focus is on His work for us. Obedience in the New Covenant comes as a result of one Man's obedience on the cross. It is no longer just about our love for Him and conjuring up this mindset of "I love God with all my heart, mind, soul, and strength," but about His love for us shown in the person of Jesus Christ in His death and resurrection. His love for us motivates us into love returned to Him. We can only love Him because He first loved us and chose us, and predestined us to be blameless and holy (see Eph. 1:4).

Being obedient is not something you do because God will smite you if you don't. Being obedient should be something you do because you love God, because He loves you. I love my wife, so I want to honor my wife. Honor out of fear of punishment is not real honor, but honor out of love and respect is. If you understand His love for you, love will overflow from your heart to Him, translating into honoring Him. When He tells you something, your desire should be to listen to Him and obey Him. Every time we disobey the leading of Holy Spirit, we slowly harden our hearts toward Him and His voice. Our ears become dull. The Bible says, "Today, if you hear My voice, don't harden your hearts like you did in the rebellion" (see Heb. 3:15). He is always speaking to us every day.

Today He is asking you not to harden your heart to His voice. Obedience is not a burden when it's motivated by love and honor. There have been times when I just didn't want to talk to someone or even give a word; I just wanted to relax. But God said, "You need to do this." Even though I don't always feel in my emotions like doing what He says, when I do, I'm always happy and see amazing Kingdom things happen.

I remember one of the first times I really felt what it was like to totally disobey something that God was speaking to me to do. I was a brand-new believer in Jesus—about nine months at the time. I had really been seeking God, and He had been speaking to me about the power of learning to recognize His voice. I had been asking God to give me detailed words for people and I wanted to be stretched and used to demonstrate His power.

I was working in landscaping at the time and one day was digging a hole underneath a shed in the back of a new residential development area. Beside where I was digging, a contractor was installing a fence. He was a relatively big guy, with lots of tattoos and piercings, and was minding his own business. All of a sudden I heard Holy Spirit say to me, *"He's got a friend named Jani. She is suicidal. Tell him to pray for her."*

I had been asking God to use me, use me, use me—yet when God spoke to me, I said, "Oh, God, please confirm it again. If You give me a confirmation that that really was You, I'll do it; I'll give the word to this man." About 15 seconds after I prayed that, the DJ on the radio that was playing in the backyard announced the next song—"Janie's Got a Gun." I was like, *What!* God tells me the guy's got a friend named Janie, she's suicidal, tell him to pray for her—and then within 15 seconds the radio announcer says the next song is "Janie's Got a Gun." What more confirmation did I need! But even though I told God I would do it if I had a confirmation, there was still a warring inside of me.

So many thoughts were in my mind. *I am a fairly new believer. What if I'm going crazy? What if I get fired?* These thoughts sound pretty ridiculous, looking back now. But I hadn't had the latest Prophetic 101 CD set or teaching on the supernatural back then. I was learning mostly as I went along. I was prolonging obedience to His word as I was pondering all these thoughts. In the Kingdom life, all the things Holy Spirit tells us to do rely on timing. We need to act in wisdom according to His timing for things He speaks to us. I knew this was my moment. Some people have heard Holy Spirit tell them things to do years ago, and they still haven't done them.

As I was prolonging this process, I kept digging the hole. My boss came and said he needed me in the front yard. I said okay and thought, *I'll give the word when I come back—100 percent.* I was so confident this time. I came back about 20 minutes later and the guy was gone. I saw him pulling out of the driveway in the front and driving down the street. I missed it. I totally missed a God-opportunity, knowing it was not a coincidence but Holy Spirit speaking to me. Honestly, I felt terrible about the situation and that I had asked God to stretch me and speak to me in that way. Then when He did, I didn't act on it on time.

The good news is there is grace; there is always grace for growth. And that was a growing experience for me. From that day on, I made a commitment to God to never do that again.

When He speaks something to you, do it.

When He speaks something to you, do it. Maybe there have been times when you have felt like you should have prayed for somebody and you didn't in that moment. Then eventually when you had the strength to do it, you couldn't find the person. There is no condemnation; you do not have to live in guilt. Be encouraged knowing that you have nothing to lose by stepping out in faith and showing the love of Jesus to someone by delivering what He speaks for you to deliver, whatever it is. I could have seen the visible love of God at work if I had given the word to that man building the fence, but I learned something valuable that day. There is such honor in obedience motivated from that amazing union and love relationship you have with Jesus Christ.

WALLS OF JUDGMENT AND CYNICISM

Sometimes we're blocked and can't receive because of mindsets influenced by previous judgments or negativity toward certain spiritual experiences or movements. Some people preach or teach that we are under grace and so don't have to do anything. That's true in part. We can rest in the fact that we've been forgiven and that we are no longer under the law of sin and death—we don't need to strive to produce anything. Yet the reality is that His grace extends to us and motivates us to lay hold of what He has promised. Those who sit doing nothing are going to see only a measure. Yes, they are under grace and God has forgiven them, which is amazing. But a revelation of grace moves us into experiencing the reality of the Kingdom and seeing the reward of obedience.

Please hear me: You don't need to do anything to impress God; what impresses God is who you are and that He sees His Son Jesus Christ in you, activating faith to believe all that He has promised.

Remember, love is not just something you say; it is represented in your actions, fueled by the Lord's love for you.

Sometimes other people's actions get in the way of our ability to see God for who He is. Often people do not enter into all that God has for them because they have judgments and critical opinions about certain experiences, movements, or manifestations of God in other people. I've seen people miss out on so much that God had for them just because they couldn't handle someone beside them shaking or laughing. It doesn't matter if you shake, bake, sit still, stand up, jump up and down, run around in circles, or are in ecstasies of the Lord. If it's truly God, you should want it. If it offends your mind, it could be one of three things: a devil's influence, discernment of the flesh, or an offense God is using to reveal your heart.

John Arnott, a minister out of Toronto, Canada, made a great statement as I heard him speak one time, saying, "God sometimes will actually offend your mind to reveal your heart." I believe this happened to John the Baptist even after he had baptized Jesus and declared that Jesus was the Lamb of God who takes away the sin of the world. John was to prepare the way of the Lord; he was a repentance preacher, a wilderness junkie. Then Jesus came. He was a carpenter, eating and drinking and hanging out with prostitutes, tax collectors, and drunks. While John was preaching repentance, Jesus was preaching that the Kingdom is at hand, healing the sick, casting out demons, raising the dead, and cleansing the lepers. When John was imprisoned, he sent two of his disciples to Jesus to ask Him if He really was the One to come. What? Didn't he know? Everything prior indicated that John did know who Jesus really was. I think with all the external manifestations that were happening, maybe John didn't totally expect things to look the way that they did.

This is the sad reality for many who are prophesying about the coming moves of God and about the emerging generation. When those things do come, often it's not the way they thought or expected, and just like John, they begin to question. Offense sets in because God didn't package it the way they thought it should be packaged. In Matthew 11:4-6 Jesus says to two of John's disciples:

> *Go and tell John the things which you hear and see: the blind see and the lame walk; the lepers are cleansed and the deaf hear; the dead are raised up and the poor have the gospel preached to them.* **And blessed** ***is he who is not offended because of Me.***

When we judge others wrongly, we actually shut the door to reaching much of our potential. Others' experiences and testimonies are our chance to believe for ourselves. Their breakthroughs have the chance to become ours if we are open. This is part of being in the Body of Christ. We all bring strength to each other even though our predominant functions and responsibilities may be radically different. If we're sowing judgment, if we're sowing negativity, if we're backbiting or gossiping, if we're criticizing, we end up closing the door of our hearts to ever walk into specific spiritual encounters with God. Thankfully, His grace is always available. Let Him love on you and guide you. Take time to repent. Get God's perspective on the situation or circumstance.

I'm very careful about what I say when it comes to certain manifestations of the Spirit. It's pretty simple to tell when it's the devil or the flesh wanting to get attention. Who wants to miss anything God has for them? People get uncomfortable and can get very judgmental very quickly, especially when it comes to moves of God and different spiritual experiences. They say things such as, "Look at that, it's all flesh, it's all demons," without taking the time to seek the Lord and the Word on the matter.

That's exactly what the religious people of the day accused Jesus of—casting out devils with a devil (see Matt. 12:24). *What? That doesn't make any sense.* Yet that's exactly what so many do today by writing blogs, creating websites, and saying things that promote division and fear within the Body of Christ.

Be careful not to reject the works of Christ and attribute them to the devil. God has broken the walls of isolation down through Christ's finished work. He's broken down the power of sin over our lives. Too many are building walls again because of their negative perspectives or lack of knowledge. When we don't understand something, especially when it comes to things of the supernatural, we often try to protect ourselves. In understanding our intimate union with Christ, let's make sure that in our perspectives and beliefs we don't disable ourselves from going as far as we can in discovering all that He is and wants to be for us. Because of this union, we have access to the greatest secret of the supernatural life, moving us into wild and crazy experiences with Him.

> *Furthermore, because* **we are united with Christ,** *we have received an inheritance from God, for he chose us in advance, and he makes everything work out according to his plan* (Ephesians 1:11 NLT).

CHAPTER 10

EXPERIENCING
THE GREATER WORKS

Most assuredly, I say to you, he who believes in Me, the works
that I do he will do also; and greater works than these he will do,
because I go to My Father. (John 14:12)

A S believers in Jesus, we are part of creating a Kingdom culture
inside and outside the four walls of the church that manifest the
great works of the Kingdom. This is Heaven's mandate and God's
heart desire. As we come into a revelation of our identity in Christ as
children of God and our purpose and position in the Kingdom, the
mountains of society will not know what hit them. We will see a day
just like Daniel saw and experienced—men and women of God in
places of influence releasing the supernatural Kingdom of Heaven into

the business world, school systems, government, media, music industry, arts, and anywhere else they find themselves.

I love when God sovereignly shows up in a special way, but if we live only out of that experience, we will miss huge opportunities to live our potential on earth in Christ. Much of Kingdom life is a choice that we make, through believing in what God says about us and about Himself. Jesus told His disciples to go:

> *And as you go, preach, saying, "The kingdom of heaven is at hand."*
> *Heal the sick, cleanse the lepers, raise the dead, cast out demons.*
> *Freely you have received, freely give* (Matthew 10:7-8).

So don't just wait for what God told you to do—you have what you need to do it. Be responsible with what He has freely given you. He gave the disciples power and authority—*dunamis* power to perform miracles and *exousia* authority to exercise it over situations and the demonic realm.

People get all hung up on statements like, "Make sure you say, 'Jesus does the healing.'" That's true and obvious. Jesus is the Healer and Source of all life. But He uses us as the channel through which His power is manifested. There are times when He does the work without anyone because He really does not need us. He chooses to use us, and what a privilege that is. Just as Jesus was the exact representation and expression of the Father, so are we to be reflections of Him on earth (see Heb. 1:3). He was the firstborn among many brethren, meaning prototype, and we are to follow that example. He is the model on which we can build our lives. And because of His model, we get to experience the greater works of the Kingdom that Jesus talked about in John 14.

CULTURALLY RELEVANT CHURCH

Relevant is one of those buzzwords flying around the Body of Christ, especially in the younger generation. The focus of what seems to be a movement of culturally relevant churches has a common thread—be cool and hip so you can attract and reach unbelievers for Jesus. This is not the core of the message that Jesus came to this earth with. What made Jesus relevant was that He was a man of supernatural power of love and grace. People are searching for spiritual truth, and we as believers in Jesus Christ have the answer. In a visual, media-driven, cosmopolitan society, we cannot be so far removed from the culture that we cannot relate. However, it is not part of the plan of Heaven to bring our church culture into the world's culture; rather, it is to bring the Kingdom to the culture of the world through His church, the Body of Christ. As a result, we will have a Kingdom culture where the King has His rule and reign on every mountain of society.

In order to reach a new culture, we must deal with our outdated, elite spiritual language.

Now, in order to reach a new culture, we must deal with our outdated, elite spiritual language. We can't go out on the streets and say, "You need to know the Lamb of God who was slain before the foundation of the world for you." Or, "His blood was shed on Calvary for you; receive it." That may make sense to the believer who's been in the church most of his or her life, but if we are going out to touch the culture—outside of an Acts 9:3 experience—we, just like Jesus at the well, need to relate to the culture with their language. Jesus was led by what He saw His Father do (see John 5:19), and it was important for Him to minister the way He did to the Samaritan woman (see John 4:1-26). He did something culturally unacceptable by the very fact that Jews did not associate with Samaritans, but culturally relevant in His language and approach, thus bringing about an encounter and revelation of who He was to this Gentile woman.

Imagine if Jesus had sat down at the well with the Samaritan woman and said, "You need the Lamb, you need My blood, you need My body for your healing. I was slain before the foundation of the world" (see Rev. 13:8). Instead, Jesus used the current situation of drawing water from the well and hid spiritual truth in it to get her attention. Then He gave her a word of knowledge, which got her attention even more. He explained what He had come to initiate as the Messiah, then left her with the revelation that He was the Messiah to come.

Language that worked 50 years ago is not going to be very productive in our culture today. In an arising new age, spiritually sensitive society, we need to be able to relate and teach spiritual truth with language that makes sense. I'm not necessarily talking about trying to change spiritual terms, but there are some people who speak completely normal—until they get behind the pulpit. Then they switch to old King James language. I don't understand this! Neither do most others. That language may have worked in times past and actually made sense, but to a whole new generation, it doesn't. The culture today has a different language; they do not speak in King James.

For many years we ministered in New Orleans during the Mardi Gras festivals. We set up "free spiritual reading booths" beside the psychics, tarot card readers, and crystal ball healers. Not only would we get the chance to minister to the people, but many who were searching for answers came and sat down with us—not realizing that we were believers in Jesus Christ with The Answer for life. Some people get their religious panties in a knot when they hear a phrase like "free spiritual readings." But we are using the language of the culture to reach the culture. Jesus is free, He is spiritual, and He reads people's hearts, knowing everything about them, and that is good theology.

If we had posted a sign, "Free Christian words of life" or "Come be washed by the blood of the Lamb," I guarantee that people would have turned away. Most people searching for spiritual truth understand what free spiritual readings are. I can't tell you how many people I have seen give their lives to Jesus, encounter His love, be instantly healed, or be delivered of things binding them just by sitting down at one of our spiritual reading booths. The story of Jesus at the well with the woman from Samaria is a perfect example of this. He used current cultural relevance and language to reach out to her. I'm not saying that we should be like the world to reach the world, but we can't be so disconnected from the culture of the world that we can't relate outside of our own narrow, churchy spiritual language.

Many times as we would minister at our booths, right beside the tarot card readers, psychics, and crystal ball healers, an agitation in the spirit would take place. That happened partly because there was a clash of kingdoms, and also because our services were free, which always created a line of waiting people. A few times the fortune-tellers got upset and told us to move because they couldn't hear or access the spirit realm, that there was a blockage. Well, of course, there was! Jesus is bigger and better than any little devil or demonic force on this earth. The Kingdom of God released into an atmosphere will mess with the channel in the spiritual realm where there is anything that does not honor the name of Jesus Christ. He is the doorway and true channel to the Father of Creation and the heavenly realms. Many of these soothsayers would move their booths because they could not operate or channel their spirits when we were near.

No longer will trendy Jesus bracelets, Christian T-shirts, fancy bumper stickers, convicting condemning tracts, and cool necklaces cut it. We need to reach out with relevance, love, and supernatural power. Let me clarify that Jesus can use and does use anything we give Him to use, but there is always a better way. Many Christians think of the rejection of their evangelism and methods as persecution and just part of the process of learning to suffer like Christ. Although some of that is true, much of what people call persecution in North America is simply rejection because of our methods. We need more common street sense in addition to having a supernatural word or demonstration of power. When approaching a group of gangster types, it's not wise to go up to them with your big, coffee table Bible, Christian T-shirt, and WWJD bracelet and say, "Hey, brethren, I'm from the church down the road, and I would like to invite you to the Bible club on Tuesdays," hand them a tract that basically says they're going to hell, and then expect them to show up to your Bible club. We need to offer what they are searching for—spiritual fulfillment, even if they don't know it. We have to realize that we are in a new day and new culture compared to even 20 years ago.

> *No longer will trendy Jesus bracelets, Christian T-shirts, fancy bumper stickers, convicting condemning tracts, and cool necklaces cut it.*

We have to understand the times and realize that the culture has changed since the Book of Acts. Cultural methods talked about in Acts work amazingly well in places around the world where the gospel has not been made known and where there is deep spiritual poverty. In fact, the way I minister in other countries is not necessarily the same way I minister in North America. In North America, because of the lackadaisical spiritual condition so many find themselves in, we need to be more strategic in how we minister to people outside of the church. Going to a street corner and yelling about how everyone is going to hell may give you a measure of success, but what about going out on a street corner and sharing the goodness, grace, and love of God and demonstrating the power of God in miracles, signs, and wonders. Or flip it—demonstrate the miraculous power of God first, then share the Source of it all.

Trust me, when a blind person can see or a deaf person can hear or someone walks out of a wheelchair because he or she is supernaturally healed, crowds will gather so you can share His love and message of grace. This has happened so many times in our ministry. A miracle pops open on the street and then people gather so I can share the love and Source of the miracle with them. You can do it too. How about putting on an art show where the glory of God is displayed, or set up a dream interpretation booth, or a free spiritual reading booth? You may think you don't have a gift for interpreting dreams. However, in the New Covenant, all believers have access to the same God of power and supernatural experiences. The Bible says in Genesis that interpretations belong to God (see Gen. 40:8). So because God is inside of you, it is in you to understand not only your dreams, but also the dreams of others. But like anything, this is something that needs to be developed over time.

Ultimately, people need to see Jesus in you operating. They need to see Him being demonstrated in word and power. The biggest part of being culturally relevant still lies in demonstrating the Spirit's power. Paul said it well when he said that he didn't come with wise and eloquent words of wisdom or speech but with a demonstration of the Spirit's power (see 1 Cor. 2:4). He did not come with an intellectual accent or try to fabricate a perfect 15-minute message that didn't offend anyone. The emphasis was on demonstrating and showcasing the resurrection power of Christ that was within him to those around.

> *The biggest part of being culturally relevant still lies in demonstrating the Spirit's power.*

What people are truly searching for is not just cool, hip gatherings—they want and need a spiritual encounter with the living God. We are most relevant when we can be the gateway for a supernatural encounter in which people experience the goodness of Jesus Christ in His grace, truth, and love. We've had people drawn to us on the street because it appeared that we were having a party. Like the Book of Acts chapter 2, the people on the outside accused them of being drunk at 9 o'clock in the morning. At times we are under the intoxicating influence of the Spirit's love and power, and people are drawn to this. As a result, many encounter Jesus and are healed and delivered.

Many who don't like this style of outreach have been attending church for years and don't seem to like anything spiritual that has the appearance of disorderly fun. I'm not saying that you have to be weird to attract people. I'm saying let His influence fall on you and let Him be the One who ultimately attracts people. Jesus is attractive to anyone who is searching for spiritual truth. Often in our meetings, there are people who come in high on drugs or drunk on alcohol—they have been drawn by the Spirit. Some may think they are there to distract, and that may happen, but something supernatural has drawn them, and I believe it's Jesus. He loves them so much and wants to set them free from addiction and pain.

JESUS—THE GREATEST EVANGELIST

As noted previously, John 5:19-20 is a perfect model for outreach. Jesus said that He only did what He saw His Father doing. In John 12:50a Jesus says, *"Whatever I speak, just as the Father has told Me, so I speak."* Jesus did what He heard His Father say and what He saw His Father do. We are called to love people the way Jesus loves people. He relayed the message based on what He saw. We just need to wait and let God show us where we are to go and/or what we are to do. We must learn to see and do only what the Father is doing. In Luke 2:49 Jesus says, *"I must be about My Father's business."* It's easy to get into the habit of doing our own thing, but we need to be about our Father's business, just as Jesus was.

Being still in the Father's presence and spending time with Him to get His heartbeat is so important if we want to hear clearly what He wants us to do. Joe Mebrahtu, one of my associates, who flows in an awesome prophetic anointing on the streets, leads the outreach component of Kingdom Culture Ministries in Ottawa, Canada. He often takes time with his team listening and hearing what God wants them to do and where He wants them to go before they go out. Every time, they see amazing healings, and people encounter the love of Jesus in the streets, malls, and coffee shops.

Years ago when I was living in the U.S., a few of us often went to a specific coffee shop to minister to people. This was a place where witches, warlocks, and satanists regularly hung out, some with lizard tongues or other interesting features. I was still a fairly new believer at this point and was really desiring to recognize the voice of God at a more intense level. One night before going, I said to God, "Bring me into a vision of what is going to happen at the coffee shop tonight." I waited in stillness before God for a few hours and then had a vision. In the vision, God told me what I would see that night. He said, "When you go to the coffee shop tonight you will see a girl in her late teens, with blonde hair, pale-looking, wearing a black shirt, and sitting at a round table. When she was five and six years old, she was abused by her father and moved from a different state in the U.S. to come here. The first letter of her first name is 'J.' Tell her I am going to heal her of the mental and emotional baggage she is still carrying because of the abuse as a child." Two and a half hours after I got to the coffee shop, I still had not seen anyone who fit that description but really was confident it had been God speaking to me. I had written it down so I would not forget the details. Eventually I noticed a round table with two people sitting at it, and one of them really fit the description. I felt this was it.

So I walked up to her with my journal in my hand and said, "I don't want to freak you out or anything, but my name is Shawn and I'm from Canada. What's your name?" She said, "My name is Jennifer." So I opened my journal and said, "I believe that God showed you to me in a vision before I came here, and I'm just going to read this to you out of my journal. If it's wrong, I'm sorry; and if it's right, awesome." I left it open. (Keep in mind I was just really discovering the word of knowledge at this point and did not really know what I was doing.)

I read out my vision and the girl began to weep. Her friend was freaked out, wondering what was going on, and said, "How do you know that? Are you a psychic?" I said, "No, I just believe that God speaks today, and that God loves you both so much that He showed some Canadian dude all these things in a vision. God loves you that much." It turned out that everything I had written down about the vision was true. She was 19 years old. She was wearing a black shirt, had blonde hair, was sitting at a round table, and had been abused by her father when she was five and six. She had moved from New York to Minneapolis and the first letter of her first name was J.

Jennifer was totally overwhelmed by the presence of God as this was all happening. As she cried, I said, "Jesus wants to heal you of that mental and emotional baggage you're still carrying from when you were a child." I prayed for her and she was totally rocked. I shared the love and message of Jesus with her and she continued to weep and said, "I want to know this Jesus." She knew He was for real because of the demonstration she had just witnessed and she gave her life to Jesus that day.

One week later, we were back at that coffee shop again and I stood on a balcony in front of about eight people sharing my testimony of what had happened to me when I was 18 years old—how God had visited me in my car on the highway and all that He had taken me out of. Jennifer was in the crowd. People seemed to be resisting, but then Jennifer spoke up and said, "This is the guy from last week that knew all about me." In that moment, all those who were listening had a revelation that Jesus was the real deal. It was such a powerful experience, just like the Samaritan woman at the well who had the revelation that Jesus was the Messiah and then went back and told her whole town what had happened. Revival broke out in that town because of her testimony (see John 4:39-42).

ON THE DRUG TRIP

I received a phone call years ago from a guy I used to know who had become a drug dealer in my city. I don't know how he got my number, but he wanted to meet with me and hear my story. He'd heard through the grapevine that I "became religious"—his words. Before I met him for coffee, I asked the Lord for insight into what He wanted to do. God told me that He was going to break some chains from his life and there would be some major breakthrough.

As I shared my testimony of what God was doing in my life, in my spirit I was asking the Lord what the key was to seeing some break-through in his life. I heard the still small voice of the Spirit say to me, "Ask him about some of the drug trips he has had because I've actually tried to speak to him, but he has no idea." He told me that things were not going very well for him. The month before, he had woken up to a gun pointed at his head. His house was raided for illegal drugs, he was arrested, and now he was waiting for a court date. He was depressed, borderline suicidal, and hadn't finished school.

When he paused, I told him what I felt the Spirit had said to me. I said, "This is weird, but I feel like God just spoke to me and said to ask you about some of the drug trips that you've had because God has actually tried to speak to you, and you didn't even know it." Just to clear the record in case you are wondering, yes, God can and often does invade—even in our ignorance—various experiences that we have self-induced, to get our attention. He will even invade moments when you have neglected Him with your actions, and this is a demonstration of His love and grace. You may be in habitual sin, but God's grace is greater and He will chase you down. He will do whatever He has to do to get your attention. He can even invade a drug trip that someone is on. God can do anything He wants to do, any way He wants to do it. I have a friend who got saved during an acid trip and was totally transformed. When this happens, an instant sobering takes place even though the body may be filled with drugs. Jesus invaded the situation by His mercy and grace because of His love for that friend, and he got totally saved.

So after I told this drug dealer what God had told me, he was absolutely shocked. He said, "I've had two specific drug trips that I haven't told anybody about because they freaked me out—they were incredibly weird." He described the first one. (Keep in mind that this young man had no grid for the church, the Bible, or anything Jesus.) He said that during the first drug-induced trip, he was in his house and he fell into a trance. He didn't call it a trance, but it was like a trance because of the description he gave me of what had happened. In this trance-like experience, he was given two options. The first option was like light and he could feel peace and joy. He said that the feeling that he had in this first option was the same feeling he experienced as I was sharing my testimony with him earlier in the conversation. He continued describing what took place in the first option. He saw a Man with blondish hair; the Man was beautiful, radiating peace and joy; and he could feel these emotions in his experience.

Then he said the scene switched, and he was given a second option. He said there was darkness. He felt fear and anxiety and was in complete and utter panic. He actually woke up in a panic, sweating profusely because of the intensity of the experience. His brother and mother happened to come into his room as this was going on and they were crying because they didn't know what to do. It looked as if he was having a convulsion or something. Immediately it was very obvious to me that God had given him two options: one was the Kingdom of light and Jesus, and the other was the kingdom of darkness and satan. He saw the realities of both worlds.

The second drug trip was three days later, and this time he was at a house party and sitting in a room by himself. All of a sudden he heard an audible voice speak to him and say, "You're going to write poems, and the poems you write will help people and bring healing." Then he saw a crown like a king would wear, and he said it felt like a king was speaking to him. Remember, he had no grid for Jesus, the King of kings.

I interpreted what I felt God was saying and ministered to him out of these two experiences. It was an awesome and powerful time. We met again a few weeks later and he asked, "Shawn, how do I find this God? How do I get to God? What do I do?" He said, "I guess I have to let some stuff go...maybe I should stop dealing drugs."

I didn't say any of that to him—he knew it from within. I said, "God will show Himself to you; God will make Himself real to you." I told him about the love of Jesus. I went back to his house with him and said that I wanted to pray for him. When I asked him if he wanted to receive Jesus, he said, "Yeah, but can I smoke one last joint first?"

The Lord said to me, "You need to pray for him before he does that because something is going to happen." I went into the garage with him and began to pray for him as he was holding the joint in his hand. All of a sudden, the power of God came all over his body, and then I heard a sound and looked down to see that he crushed the joint in his hand. He said he felt electricity go all through his body. Then he said he wouldn't need the drugs anymore and threw the joint in the garbage.

Moments later, he gave his life to Jesus Christ as he encountered Him in the garage. We walked back into his house, and I watched him flush all his hard drugs down the sink. Then he walked over to his CD collection and said, "I guess I can't be listening to this anymore." The Lord was all over him; it was so wild. "But there's just one problem," he said. "I'm supposed to meet this guy in an hour because he's coming to buy some drugs, and now I have no drugs left. He's coming from far away, so he's already left. Can you come with me?"

I said, "Yes." The whole scenario felt like it was out of a movie. Because I had been in that world in my life at one point, I was not scared. I understood it. We walked to an area by some train tracks. A nice white truck pulled up, and an older man walked out into the middle of the field near the tracks. When both of them came together I heard my friend say to the one wanting to buy drugs, "I have no drugs for you...this is it...I'm not doing this anymore. It's what's best for me."

It was all so amazing to see the Kingdom at work in this young man. One conversation and listening to the still small voice sparked a whirlwind of supernatural experience with Jesus.

THE PURPOSE OF PROPHETIC EVANGELISM

Prophetic evangelism is simply being led by the Spirit outside the four walls of the church, just like Jesus was all the time. This seems to be another one of those charismatic buzzwords that have this mystical nature attached to it. Instead it is so simple—it simply is the by-product of the Spirit-led life.

Prophetic evangelism is simply being led by the Spirit outside the four walls of the church.

The purpose of prophetic evangelism is to speak destiny and truth over people. Many people don't know what God thinks about them, so we need to go out there and tell them. We need to bring the true prophetic into the midst of all the false. I have walked into psychic shops and ministered to psychics and have actually given them money so I can give them a word. I tell them, "I'll give you money so I can give you a word. I want to bless you. If you let me give you a word, I'll give you some money." That always surprises them.

One time I was flying back from a ministry trip in Newfoundland, Canada. There was a woman sitting beside me who was flying to a psychic fair to have her dreams interpreted. *What a divine setup,* I thought to myself. I told her that Jesus speaks and He could tell me what her dreams mean. "Tell them to me," I said. She was shocked. But I know that interpretations belong to God (see Gen. 40:8) and that the Big Fella and I are connected. After she told me her dreams, God gave me profound interpretations for her concerning them. She was deeply impacted and said, "Now I don't have to go to that fair. I just got everything that I was going to the fair for." What she was really looking for was Jesus and didn't even know it. He is the true Source for spiritual understanding and clarity. This is a prime example of why we as the Body of Christ need to be trained and equipped in the supernatural.

Many times when operating this way outside on the street we quickly realize that it is not only for the nonbeliever but also for the believer who may need some encouragement. I can't tell you how many times we have run into this and have been able to encourage believers who may be struggling with their faith during our street outreaches.

Years ago when I was living in Alaska, my team and I set up a free spiritual reading booth at a local coffee shop. Remember, we used this language because we knew people would understand it. This was our first time doing this specific kind of outreach. We talked to the manager and said we would do it for free and that it would bring them business by drawing in crowds. The manager agreed, and that is exactly what happened. I really had no idea what I was doing, but we stepped out in faith believing God would move and speak through us. We advertised it all over the community. The place was so packed there was standing room only. We had three or four teams of two or three people who sat at various tables and ministered to people one by one, as well as in couples. We prophesied over people for four and a half hours straight.

It was wild. People were healed, saved, and set free. The one thing that shocked me was that so many believers came. The sad thing is that on our flyer and ad we purposely did not mention Jesus. Our purpose and goal was not to reach out to believers but nonbelievers, to show them the love and reality of Jesus Christ when they came. Don't get me wrong; it was amazing to be able to strengthen and encourage those who already had a relationship with Jesus Christ, but something was incredibly wrong with this picture. Clearly, for all they knew, we could have been tarot card readers, psychics, or mediums. This told me that believers in Jesus Christ are hungry for the supernatural and for direction—and they are not going to the Body of Christ or Jesus Himself. Christ working through His church needs to be the main source for the things of the supernatural. We need to model what Daniel and his three friends stood for and be the leading force in society in this area (see Dan. 1:20).

To the nonbeliever, we need to be the example of the truth. Paul wrote in Romans 10:14:

> *How then shall they call on Him in whom they have not believed?*
> *And how shall they believe in Him of whom they have not heard?*
> *And how shall they hear without a preacher?*

If you don't go, how are they going to know the truth of who Jesus really is? There are many people in our culture who have never heard the true gospel of Jesus. They've heard a gospel, but it's a message of religion and of good works that produces bondage fueled by condemnation.

Hebrews 5:14 says, *"But solid food belongs to those who are of full age, that is, those who by reason of use have their senses exercised to discern both good and evil."* If we are going to become seasoned in this kind of supernatural lifestyle, we have to step out and do the stuff Jesus promises we can do if we just believe. We can go through all the training. We can go through all the memorization. We can have all the tracts we want. But until we do it, we will not mature in it. We must be seasoned and wise in discerning what is of God and what is not. The specific context of this Scripture in Hebrews 5 relates to sound doctrine; the principle applies to our practical everyday spiritual life. Like anything we grow in, we need to use what we have. It's by reason of use that we develop our skills and gifts.

Reach out. Have a conversation with a stranger. Give someone an anointed smile. For some this is a good first step to reaching out with the love of Jesus. Drop off some drive-by, drive-thru "Jesus Loves You" bombshells at your local fast food restaurants. Don't worry, you are protected in your car from being stoned. In all seriousness, start where your faith and grace level is. Don't feel like you have to have a detailed word of knowledge and prophetic word for someone in the beginning. If it's hard for you to say, "Jesus loves you," then how are you going to step out in a detailed word of knowledge telling someone his age, the color of his car, and his name? Take baby steps because you still may be drinking milk. Some people need a longer process because they have been conditioned a certain way for a long time. Let me remind you, though, that one encounter with Jesus can trump all of that. In my early walk with God, I had a really amazing encounter with a man on a street all because I complimented his shirt. And he had an encounter with Jesus. The compliment opened a door for a supernatural breakthrough in his life. The more you practice and step out with God, the more you are able to sense and discern what is and what is not God.

SHARING OUR FAITH

We will have a greater understanding of all the good things we have in Christ when we share our faith with others. In relaying His heart in reaching those who do not know Him, we come into a greater revelation of His heart and mind.

There is something about sharing our faith with others. It started to happen to me at a very early time in my spiritual walk. I noticed I was growing in my faith exponentially at an accelerated pace. The power of God follows us as we share the message of the gospel. We grab hold of the heart of Jesus at a whole new level when we share freely the message of the gospel of Jesus Christ. What's the point of the Kingdom life if we are never going to share the reality of Jesus and His power with someone else?

Yes, we are blessed, we have our ticket to Heaven, and we can have a relationship with God on the earth now, but there is so much more. It's the extension of our relationship with Him to love those who don't know the message of love and grace. I believe one of the reasons we actually mature and our faith is strengthened through sharing our faith with others, is that our spirit man grows through perseverance because of the discouragement and frustration we experience at times. We will question things like, *Why didn't this person get healed after I prayed for her? I believe what Jesus said about healing, I know what the Scriptures say about healing, so why didn't this person get healed?* This is part of the faith walk. We don't live by sight but by faith. Faith that's persistent will see, but the Kingdom is not like instant coffee. You don't mix it with water and there you have it.

Scripture likens the Kingdom of Heaven to a mustard seed (see Mark 4:30-32). Time is one of the determining components to harvest, as there is always seedtime and harvest (see Gen. 8:22): *"And let us not grow weary while doing good, for in due season we shall reap if we do not lose heart"* (Gal. 6:9). There were times when I was very discouraged after being on the street or after leading a service because of one person who didn't encounter Jesus or get healed. So many others did, and yet there was that question to God, *Why?* But to keep going and not give up is the heart of Heaven for you. These processes of life deepen your understanding of the Lord and build your trust in Him.

You and I need to go. It's so important. If you want to experience a supernatural life, then go after the thing that we are all called to as believers in Jesus. That's the sharing of the message of love and grace— the gospel message. Power follows you in the go. So go make yourself available and watch what happens, remembering this all flows from a place of knowing Him. And that's the secret of the supernatural life.

CALLING ALL DANIELS

J UDE 22-23 says, *"And on some have compassion, making a distinction; but others save with fear, pulling them out of the fire, hating even the garment defiled by the flesh."* The New International Version says, *"Be merciful to those who doubt; snatch others from the fire and save them; to others show mercy, mixed with fear—hating even the clothing stained by corrupted flesh."*

There is a growing post-modern, supernatural spiritual movement. This movement is comprised of people who know that Jesus is relevant. He is the One who crosses all boundaries, races, styles, tongues, tribes, denominations, and sects. He trumps everything that we think is important; He trumps it all. The message of the Kingdom is a relevant message, even though the expression of it may change through the generations. It's a message of confrontation with love and power.

The message of the Kingdom is not, "I want to get to know you for two years and have a relationship with you before I tell you about Jesus Christ and of His love and power to set you free." No. Some call this approach discernment and wisdom. Jesus would probably call it fear and pride.

We have no idea what may happen to us tomorrow—we must seize the day and moment. We can't afford to miss one more God-opportunity because of fear of losing a relationship or fear of rejection. Maybe you don't want to offend people. Maybe the gospel has been dummied down to an intellectual, cool Christian club. If you study the life of Jesus, you will notice that most of the people He offended were the religious folk. He didn't offend the lost and dying, even though some of His methods for the miraculous seemed weird, even outrageous. People with religious baggage are more easily offended than anyone else it seems, both today and back when Jesus walked the earth.

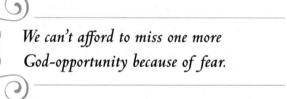

We can't afford to miss one more God-opportunity because of fear.

I was speaking one Sunday morning on impartation, knowing that there were many unbelievers in the room. Even for many believers, teaching on the truth and power of impartation can be foreign and not totally understood, let alone for those who had never been to church or in that kind of environment before. I could have assessed the situation with my mind and thought, *What I'm saying seems so out there and irrelevant to where many people are at in this room.* But I knew it was what Holy Spirit wanted me to do.

Many people got saved in that service, but there were two drug addicts who got totally rocked by the power and love of Jesus. They may or may not have understood in their minds what I was talking about, but their spirits were impacted and they encountered Jesus in a mighty way. As I was ministering to one of them, I said she was about to experience the buzz of Heaven in her body, and that drugs or alcohol couldn't compare to God's real, tangible power. Drug addicts understand words like that more than "the glory of God" or "the oil of joy." As I put my hand on her head, the power of God came all over her. She began to shake and cry. Later her response was, "I've done a lot of hard drugs in my life, but I've never experienced anything like that." Jesus knew she needed a supernatural encounter with His presence that would seal all that He had already done in her heart in that service.

The Spirit will always do the work in the end. Our calling is to listen to Holy Spirit's method. Some of the most practical wisdom that we try to walk in to reach people is God's version of foolishness. What may seem foolish to us is actually God's wisdom. Often what is illogical to us is logical to God.

In the midst of aiming to be relevant to the culture as a church, we cannot water down the message of the Kingdom. Don't be afraid to rock the boat a little bit when it comes to your approach to reaching out to people. Don't think you have to know them for a couple of years before you can tell them about the love of Jesus Christ. We can't think that one day, after we've built up enough trust in the individual, we can just pop in a little Jesus truth into the conversation and hope all is well.

What are you going to do when you get to Heaven one day and see standing in the non-Heaven line all of your neighbors and others you never talked to about Jesus because you were waiting for the right time? At that point it's too late; you can't do anything. Sometimes you have to aggressively snatch them from the fire. Like it says in Jude 22-23, you have to go after their souls and say, "Listen, hell wasn't created for you, but Heaven was. Let me tell you about God's grace and love for you. In fact, let me pray for you so you can experience Him right now!"

I had a dream not too long ago that I was in hell. I experienced what it felt like to be totally separated from God. It was worse than I ever imagined. Not only did I feel what it was like to be separated from God for myself, but I also felt how my kids and all those closest to me would feel being in that place of separation. It was the most horrible feeling imaginable.

In my dream, hell was called "the deep" because the depth of the pain and darkness was so great. I could not think of anything good— no matter how hard I tried. That's what hell is. There is nothing good. It is pure death. There's no fruit of the Spirit in hell. I was trying to find something to numb the pain. I was trying to recall memories that would bring joy. But no, I could not access anything good or joyful. I tried to make myself smile, but even this small act was impossible. The muscles in my face were unable to make a smile. It was a horrible feeling. My memory of good things was totally erased. When I awoke, I knew what it would be like to be totally separated from God.

Having an encounter like this in a dream brings a whole new perspective on the importance of bringing the message of Jesus to a lost and dying world. My prayer for you is that you will allow these secrets of the supernatural life outlined in this book to take root in your spiritual walk with Jesus and that the experience of His supernatural Kingdom would become the norm for you. Stay enamored with Jesus Christ as He is *your gateway to supernatural experiences* in this life, and forever after. Through this book you have just uncovered many of the secrets of the supernatural life. Use them, and watch what He does in you and through you!

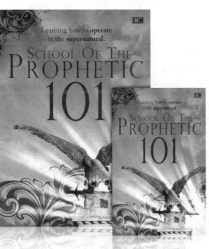

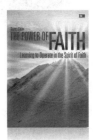

IN THE RIGHT HANDS, THIS BOOK WILL CHANGE LIVES!

Most of the people who need this message will not be looking for this book. To change their lives, you need to put a copy of this book in their hands.

> *But others (seeds) fell into good ground, and brought forth fruit, some a hundred-fold, some sixty-fold, some thirty-fold* (Matthew 13:8).

Our ministry is constantly seeking methods to find the good ground, the people who need this anointed message to change their lives. Will you help us reach these people?

> *Remember this—a farmer who plants only a few seeds will get a small crop. But the one who plants generously will get a generous crop* (2 Corinthians 9:6).

EXTEND THIS MINISTRY BY SOWING
3 BOOKS, 5 BOOKS, 10 BOOKS, **OR MORE TODAY,**
AND BECOME A LIFE CHANGER!

Thank you,

Don Nori Sr., Founder
Destiny Image
Since 1982

DESTINY IMAGE PUBLISHERS, INC.

"Promoting Inspired Lives."

VISIT OUR NEW SITE HOME AT
WWW.DESTINYIMAGE.COM

FREE SUBSCRIPTION TO DI NEWSLETTER

Receive free unpublished articles by top DI authors, exclusive
discounts, and free downloads from our best and newest books.
Visit www.destinyimage.com to subscribe.

Write to: Destiny Image
            P.O. Box 310
            Shippensburg, PA 17257-0310

Call: 1-800-722-6774

Email: orders@destinyimage.com

For a complete list of our titles or to place an order
online, visit www.destinyimage.com.

FIND US ON FACEBOOK OR FOLLOW US ON TWITTER.

www.facebook.com/destinyimage   facebook
www.twitter.com/destinyimage   twitter